MW00879905

Clued In London

The Concise and Opinionated Guide to the City

Dean Dalton + Andie Easton

Senior Editors:
Richard Soto, Alan Duke

Contributing Photographers:
Moyan Brenn, Alán Duke, Richard Soto, Robert Whitrow
Contributed photos edited by L. Osterhoudt

Logo created by Scooter Reyes

The world is a big place unless you know where to look.

The Clued In Travel Team

London, England

Travel is back and we couldn't be happier! The city is looking fantastic and your visit here will be even better than you can imagine with this brand new edition of *Clued In London.* It is quite simply your key to a truly wonderful trip.

Ah London, how can we best describe you? You're a metropolis with a past, and what a past it was... royal, regal, literary, powerful, and extremely proper. Your manners somehow set the standard for the rest of the civilized world. But you have been bloody too, ruthless to a fault in order to stand by your beliefs. Your river still flows mightily through the heart of your present day city but only God knows how many skulls lurk there, moving gently in the undercurrents. Many beheadings concluded with the traitor's head being tossed into the Thames from the riverbank near the bloody Tower.

Can today's visitors enjoy such a place? Absolutely! You might even lose your mind over it, which is much better than loosing your head. London relishes its past, but has made amazing (*heh hem*) headway into today's modern world. It's suddenly a great food capital – something it was not able to boast twenty years ago. Make certain you arrive with an appetite because our dining recommendations are awesome. Wonderful new restaurants have popped up everywhere. Even the Food Halls at Harrods and tasty stalls of the crowded Borough Market will make you swoon with culinary delight.

London is a sprawling city and is separated into distinct neighborhoods, each with its own vibe and style. The most important, historical spots have been somewhat encroached upon and will have to be sought out. The original "old London" area is called *The City*, and along with a section of *Westminster* has all the historical sights. But there's much more to London than this. Much more. That's why we'll be helping you make the best use of the Underground tube trains and Black Cabs. You'll need them to get around, especially if Uber loses its current London contract.

Don't miss an evening at the Royal Opera House, or take in some musical theatre or an offbeat play in the West End. Explore Chinatown, or see the official state rooms at Buckingham Palace if The King is not in residence. There are parks and squares galore, and so many cool galleries and museums that choosing which to visit can be difficult. *To visit the wax museum or not to visit the wax museum?* And between all the shopping and dining we believe one could stay in London for a year and not tire of any of it. Make sure to bring a travel-friendly debit or credit card because this city has suddenly become virtually cash-free (as in no cash allowed/plastic only.) But more on that later...

We love the Victoria & Albert Museum with its vast collection of decorative art and memorabilia. We love the Tower of London with its breathtaking display of the actual Crown Jewels, and never hesitate to take City Cruises' relaxing and informative Thames river tour. At night we recommend taking a cab to Nightjar, a lounge with decidedly unusual cocktails. Dare we say they have the most creative cocktails in the world? Indeed. Then there are the side trips out of the city, each in there own way distinct and unforgettable.

But as fabulous as London is, its immense size can pose a problem if you arrive without a plan and have no clue as to what is worth spending money on or not. Our chapters are literally broken down as **Not to be missed**, **Try to fit it in**, and **Skip it unless it's your thing** for this very reason. For the traveler on the move who does not have a month to spend there, this guide will be invaluable. Go and find your own London, tailored to your likes and interests, for this is a city that holds a different experience for each person.

As we clue you in, we hope you'll find wisdom and even some humor in our pages.

-Dean and Andie, and the entire *Clued In* team

The grandeur of Tower Bridge never fails to impress

Clued In London

Getting a Clue	1
London Neighborhoods	7
Before You Leave Home	10
PART 1 – Not to be Missed	13
PART 2 – Try to Fit it in	47
PART 3 – Skip it unless it's your Thing	75
PART 4 – Feasting	91
PART 5 – The Pub Report	117
PART 6 – Treats	123
PART 7 – Accommodations	137
PART 8 – All Transport	153
PART 9 – Some Final Clues	169
From the Authors	184

Getting a Clue

Hi there. You're about to explore the most concise city guide you've ever come across. One may ask, "Can a guide book have too much information?" Yes, it can. Not everyone wants to sift through pages and pages of city history and analysis of its roadways, population growth, and how a building's bricks were laid.

You won't have that problem here. This guide is as easy to use as it is to follow, and below are some basic tips so that you can start investigating everything this 2300-year-old city has to offer. We'll help you decide what to see based on the amount of time you have in this incredible place. After the sights and a few amazing excursions, you'll find our heartfelt recommendations for restaurants, bars, nightclubs, and hangouts. After that are some notes on hotels, followed by some helpful info on transportation, festivals, special events, and basic safety.

Each entry will provide you with an *at-a-glance* layout of the most necessary details such as the days they are closed, their website address, and interesting highlights that we think you should know. The restaurants even have a rating on the ambience and noise level so you can choose precisely the right vibe you're in the mood for.

As you read on, you'll notice short bullet points labeled *Pro Tip*, *Good Advice*, *Mealtime Clue*, etc., along with an occasional personal message from us to help give you insight. Don't skip over these points; they're rich with information that will set you apart from other travelers. Here are some good clues to start with…

For fun, up-to-the-minute suggestions, visit our London page at: **www.cluedintravelbooks.com**

When to go: The mid-season months are best for getting the most out of London. The crowds are somewhat diminished and you get the added benefit of lower hotel rates which are hiked up for the summer. Even the airfares are better. Summertime in London is blessed with warmer weather, July being the warmest of all. Rain is always a threat however, especially in October, so be sure to pack an umbrella. (Fog in London is mainly a myth so don't let it concern you.) Plan your visit during a special festival or event that interests you, of which there are many. We give an overview of the most popular ones in Part 9. Visiting during these local celebrations can be good or bad depending on your outlook. While they do cause a peak in crowds and may cause hotel rates to increase, you'll undoubtedly have special memories from them.

Location, location, location. We believe that the location of your accommodation is paramount. Better to stay at a more humble place in the city center than to stay at a fancy resort that's five miles out of town. Unless you're in the thick of it, you haven't really experienced it. In London, we prefer accommodations near the River Thames and not too far from the ultra-charming Covent Garden neighborhood. It's as central as you can get and has shopping and dining galore. Just remember that London is a city of neighborhoods, each with its own distinct personality and vibe; stay in the one that suits you best and then use the Underground Tube train or a taxi when necessary.

It's never too early to think about your passport. If you need one, it will take awhile so apply for one ASAP. If you already have one, make certain the expiration date will be more than six months from the last day of your planned visit. The United Kingdom has strict rules.

Map it. The maps on your smart phone are more accurate and detailed than any we could hope to include here. Use them, and learn how they move with you. And if you don't want to be bothered finding a connection as you walk around, just take screen shots beforehand of the neighborhoods you intend to explore and view them as an expandable photo whenever you want, and with no connection needed.

The London Pass gets you a discount on some transportation as well as on sights throughout the city. If you absolutely will be visiting sights like Westminster Abbey, the Tower of London, and the

London Bridge Experience, the Pass can be a good value. The best thing about having one is that it almost always speeds you and your party to the front of the line or at least allows you to skip the ticket-buying queue altogether. This is a timesaver to be sure. Visit **www.londonpass.com** to learn more about it. If you are mostly a museum-goer then you will not need this pass; all of London's best museums and galleries are free. *In Part 9, we list all of the free museums so you can see for yourself.*

Christmastime: Most of London's sights and museums are closed from December 24 through Dec 26, and even the die-hard ones are closed on Christmas Day. There's no Underground train service on that day either, and most restaurants are shut tight. If you're timing your visit for Christmastime you might want to take this into account and add a few more days onto your stay.

Planning your trip using the internet: We have found that the more you plan beforehand, the smoother and more successful your visit will be. This includes reservations for your hotel, your rental car, your tours, some sights, and even your nightly meal. Without planning and reservations, you'll not get into the most delicious restaurants, and the best sights will already be booked up. These days this can all be easily accomplished on the internet weeks in advance, and with confirmation numbers in-hand you can hit the ground running. *Clued In London* gives you all the websites you need in order to plan an unforgettable stay in the UK.

Using your cell phone for calls within London has become easy with 4G and 5G capability. Call your carrier service before your trip to make sure you are covered abroad and for basic instructions on when and how to turn on the roaming feature. For calls within the UK, note that you'll have to add a "020" before the local eight digit phone number. Some cell phones help you out with this automatically.

About that WiFi... Smart phones and tablets are increasingly important to the traveler. They provide a convenient link to loved ones at home, as well as a wealth of information on London via the internet. For this reason, choose a hotel with free WiFi. If you ever find that it's not free, indicate that you'll not book the room unless it will be free and then watch it magically disappear. This works most of the time because it costs them nothing to comp it to you.

Fahgettaboutit. These days, especially in London, you can forget about bringing large backpacks, oversized bags, and especially luggage of any kind into their museums, palaces, galleries, and theatres. Most websites now list the maximum measurements of items allowed inside any particular venue.

Accessibility for visitors with limited mobility is extraordinarily common in London. Look for our *Stair Scare* warnings throughout this book so that we can get you easily from place to place.

Pharmacies are very easy to find. Take note of them in the area of your accommodations in case you feel unwell and need to purchase a cure. They all carry the latest products, many of which are homeopathic. Unlike their European counterparts, they are not marked with any special symbol or signage.

Voltage: Unlike the United States, the UK has 230 electrical voltage as well as a unique socket and plug style. *Your US plug will not fit into London's sockets.* Yes, that means even the charging cable for your smart phone. Since most electronic items are dual voltage, your main worry will be these sockets. For a few dollars online, you can buy a *US to UK plug adapter* that will enable your US plug to fit into the local electrical sockets.

London's nightlife is yours to discover. This town has a wide range of diversions at night, many of which are changing constantly. We offer some performance recommendations but your hotel concierge will be able to give you the most up-to-the-moment info on local entertainment.

The tap water here is fresh, clean, and safe to drink, even at the public drinking fountains.

Regarding your arrival at the airport or train station: Do not accept the car services of a private citizen, no matter how professional or persuasive they might seem. Take only the official Black Cabs in the taxi queue just outside the terminal. There are also comfortable and inexpensive bus lines that await you. (Details in the chapter titled All Transport)

London Neighborhoods

Today's London is a merger of two distinct areas, *The City of London* (now a financial center) and *The City of Westminster*. The latter is huge and made up of many diverse neighborhoods, each with their own character.

Covent Garden: This central neighborhood is completely charming and overflowing with market squares, shops, restaurants and street performers, especially in the area behind the Royal Opera House.

Mayfair: East of Hyde Park, this sophisticated Bourgeoisie neighborhood boasts fine townhouses and upscale restaurants, such as the semi-private *Sketch*. You'll also find chic hotels like Claridge's and The Soho Hotel.

Marylebone: Situated just above Mayfair, this neighborhood has more of a village feel and is home to Madame Tussauds wax Museum.

Shoreditch: North of *The City*, this hipster area emerged from a blue collar worker neighborhood of factories and work houses. It is home to Spitalfields Market, the fabulous Nightjar Speakeasy, and many vintage shops.

Knightsbridge: South of Hyde Park, this upscale area is home to luxury stores Harrods and Harvey Nichols, as well as the Victoria and Albert Museum.

Chelsea: Hugging the Thames in the area southwest of Hyde Park, Chelsea is an affluent residential area centered around King's Street. It is also home to the Chelsea Psychic Garden.

Belgravia: Squeezed in-between Chelsea and the lush grounds of Buckingham Palace, this was once the playground of the rich in the late 19th century.

Soho: Just east of Mayfair, this is London's main shopping area with a few theatres thrown in for good measure. It boasts some quaint streets in an area called Carnaby, and also includes Chinatown and most of the LGBTQ clubs and bars.

Fitzrovia: Just north of Soho, this small neighborhood boasts fun galleries and cafés.

Bloomsbury: Students and tourist rule this Georgian neighborhood which is home to the British Museum.

St. James's: This small area with the weird spelling lies between Buckingham Palace and Piccadilly Circus and has some of London's best specialty shops. It makes up a part of the famed *West End*.

Holborn: East of Covent Garden, this neighborhood has housed historic law offices and the Royal Courts as long as anyone can remember. It also boasts several fine jewelry shops.

South Bank and Southwark: These two side-by-side neighborhoods hug the River Thames along on its southern bank. This means you'll find there the London Eye wheel, Shakespeare's Globe Theatre, the Tate Modern, and the crowded but tasty Borough Market.

Notting Hill: Situated northwest of Hyde Park, this charming residential neighborhood provides easy access for the famed Portobello Road weekend antiques market as well as one very famous blue door.

Camden Town: North of Regents Park, this unusual part of London has a canal, houseboats, and more than a few funky shops.

Paddington: London's most famous train station can be found in this area north of Hyde Park.

Hyde Park: This lush green-space is simply gorgeous and is home to the Kensington Gardens and Kensington Palace, former childhood home of Queen Victoria, as well as William and Kate and their children.

The City: Once called simply *London*, this is where today's financial district has encroached upon the tiny fabled streets of Fagan and the Artful Dodger. It is home to the Tower of London, gorgeous Tower Bridge, and the Whitechapel area of Jack the Ripper.

Before You Leave Home
[A Basic Checklist]

Make sure your passports are not within six months of expiring.
Yes this is a problem. Your passports must have at least six months left before expiring, measured from your return date to the US. Some countries allow three months, but don't risk it.

Take a photo with your smart device (or make a copy to take with you) of your passport's info page.
If you lose it, this will be invaluable.

Make sure your airplane seats are confirmed.
Do this as early as possible to get the best choices.

Get £30 *from a US bank* before you travel, just to have some money on you.
Your best exchange rate will come from a banking institution's ATM in Great Britain.

Call your banking and credit card companies in the days before you depart.
Let them know your travel dates and cities; recently some banks stopped needing this information but it never hurts.

Go online to print out a suggested packing list.
You won't believe all the things you were going to forget, like those plug adaptors!

Measure your luggage in three directions and check your airline's guidelines online.
Then weigh it once it's packed; a bathroom scale works fine.

Check in online to secure your intent to board.
Most airlines allow online check-in 24 hours before the flight time.

Check your airline's terminal number so you don't end up in the wrong place.
This happens more than you know.

Pack a few small adhesive bandages just in case.
They don't take up any extra room, and having something like this in your toiletries bag can save you precious time should they be needed. Never pack brand new walking shoes for a trip like this; break them in first!

Airlines usually forbid full sizes of toiletries in your carry-on luggage.
Pack travel-sized minis of 100 ml. (3.4 oz.) or less of sunscreens, lotions, perfumes, toothpaste and mouthwash.

Prescription medications should also be packed into your carry-on luggage.
"Checked" baggage can go missing, if even for a day or two.

PART 1

[Not to be Missed]

The historical importance of the Tower of London cannot be overstated

Tower of London
[The seat of England's royal history]

Officially called His Majesty's Royal Palace and Fortress of the Tower of London, the white stone tower in the middle of this walled complex was built in 1066 under orders of William the Conqueror. It's difficult to imagine something lasting so well for nearly a thousand years but lasted it has, and has been in continuous use for the entire time.

Its role in the history of the Royal Monarchy itself cannot be understated, and for that reason alone is not-to-be-missed. Many famous traitors –some innocent, some not– died on the tower grounds, most after a very public beheading. Some of their names are quite well known and others perhaps not, but all had a story to tell... Queen Anne Boleyn, Queen Jane Grey and her husband Guildford Dudley, Queen Catherine Howard, and Sir Walter Raleigh, to name just a few.

Other royals merely sought protection in the tower, like the "White Queen" Elizabeth Woodville, and later her two sons (from Edward IV) who were taken there in 1483 but then never seen again. Even Elizabeth I was imprisoned there for a time by her own sister, Mary I.

If all of this has your head spinning, never fear! Real "Beefeater" Yeoman Warders (who are appointed by the Monarch to guard the Tower) do a great job of taking visitors on a frightening and sometimes humorous tour of the grounds every half hour. Feel free to join up with one of these groups; it will enrich your visit there.

All visitors are welcome to go inside to explore the many buildings, including the main structure which boasts the actual armor of King Henry VIII from when he was thin and when he was fat. In another building there's a display of the types of torture devices used over the years, and you can even enter the lovely chapel of St. Peter ad Vincula where the more important traitors are now resting peacefully.

We mention such things because while you're visiting the Tower you may notice a distinctly oppressive and peculiar feeling that seems to hang in the very air there. Somehow its spirit isn't a joyful one, but then how could it be? If you feel it coming on, shake off the doldrums and enter the large building next to the chapel. This is where the crown jewels of the British Monarchy are proudly displayed; just the thing to cheer you up.

www.hrp.org.uk/tower-of-london

Entry tickets can be purchased ahead on the website above to avoid their long ticket queues.

Intl. calling: (011) 44-20 3166 6000
Local landline calling: 3166 6000
Local mobile calling: 020 3166 6000

Located on Tower Hill near the Thames River,
-in The City, London

Open most days
Closed on Christmas Eve, Christmas Day, December 26 & New Year's Day

Special events throughout the year may result in sporadic closures.

Historical Highlight:

The six captive ravens of the tower are an important part of English folklore. Since the 1600's it has been believed that if the ravens ever leave the Tower then the Kingdom will fall. Britain isn't taking any chances and has several on order with a Somerset breeder at all times.

Dean says,

"The Tower of London is a World Heritage UNESCO site as well as an official royal residence of His Majesty The King."

Andie says,

"If you plan on taking a guided tour cruise on the River Thames then you should do it on the same day as your Tower visit... City Cruises is located on the riverbank in front of the castle complex. Details about their boats can be found later in this chapter."

Stair Scare:

This historic site is unable to accommodate those with limited mobility.

Mealtime Clues:

Recharge with a snack or lunch right in the Tower complex at their New Armouries Café. There's also the convenient Tower Bridge Café with outdoor tables located between the Tower and the waterfront. It's perfect for a quick bite before boarding a tour boat. For something a bit nicer, visit the Paul Patisserie right there inside the large building on the quay.

Westminster Abbey
[England's place of royal coronation and tombs]

If you can spot the tall Big Ben clock tower then you're very near Westminster Abbey. It's just a block or two north of it. We can't overstate the importance of the abbey, where kings and queens have been crowned, married, and entombed. It looks like a cathedral but is technically not one, nor is it a true abbey either. Even so, it's an important part of the Church of England. If you're into Tudor history then you must see Henry VII's Lady Chapel where a large part of the most infamous royal family is enshrined. It's at the farthest end from the main entrance.

Recently they've installed something new to see. The Abbey's breathtakingly beautiful 13th century *triforium* attic has been transformed into a gallery space and opened up to the public for the first time in seven-hundred years. Items on display pertain to the Abbey's thousand-year history as well as to Queen Elizabeth II. It is known as the Queen's Diamond Jubilee Galleries. This space sits fifty-two feet above the Abbey and can be reached by way of the Weston Tower, included with your visit.

There's just something about being inside Westminster Abbey, surrounded by all that majesty. Reserve a time slot online and purchase your tickets before your trip. Special guided tours are also available for an extra fee.

You are surrounded by history at the Abbey, not like a museum where it's just displayed, but here you are standing where history has happened.

www.westminster-abbey.org

Pre-booked, timed reservations are encouraged but not required
Their scheduled religious services are free but you must book a time online beforehand

Located at the south side of Parliament Square
-in Westminster, London
Just off of Broad Sanctuary Street

Intl. calling: (011) 44-20 7222 5152
Local landline calling: 7222 5152
Local mobile calling: 020 7222 5152

Open several days a week to visitors with reservations
Check their online calendar for your dates

Historical Highlight:

The Abbey is dated from between 960 AD to 1060 AD and all of Henry VIII's reigning offspring are buried here: Edward VI, Mary I, and Elizabeth I. (The infamous Henry himself is resting inside St. George's Chapel, at Windsor Castle.)

Dean says,

"The signage is fairly poor inside the abbey, especially in the Lady Chapel where one needs it to be exceptional. Do yourself a favor and Google a chart of this chapel so that you'll know what you're looking at when you get there. The truth is you could miss the tombs of Queen Elizabeth I and Queen Mary I without a map of some kind because they are actually in a separate section of the Lady Chapel."

Andie says,

"Please note that Westminster Abbey is not the same place as Westminster Cathedral. They are not even near each other."

Mealtime Clue:

There is a modern, casual eatery right on the premises. The Cellarium Café & Terrace is in the very location where monks used to gather for their meals back in the day. You'll find it right through the cloisters, before you exit the abbey.

Some Stair Scare:

There are parts of the Abbey which are definitely accessible to those with limited mobility. Use the ramped entrance at the north door to enter, or just ask the ticket-checkers at the front of the building. The new Queen's Diamond Jubilee Galleries are fully accessible, by elevator.

Royal Opera House
[Treat yourself to a performance]

Whether you're a fan of opera and ballet or not, the Royal Opera House never fails to impress. Rebuilt in 1852 after a devastating fire, it's usually referred to as simply performances at Covent Garden and evokes the see-and-be-seen horseshoe shape with no less than five levels of seating to choose from.

World-class productions by the incredible Royal Ballet and Royal Opera are showcased continuously throughout the year. Their website provides many video clips so that you can easily decide what to see. The dress codes have lately become more relaxed so don't fret. If you don't want to spend money on a performance then take the one-hour-fifteen minute self-tour, available on certain calendar days. Both the tour and the performances must be booked weeks ahead to avoid disappointment.

www.roh.org.uk

Purchasing tickets ahead online is required for most performances
A wide range of prices are available depending on the seat, the event, and the day

Ticket information: (011) 44-20 7304 4000
Local landline calling: 7304 4000
Local mobile calling: 020 7304 4000

Located at Bow and Russell Streets
-in Covent Garden, London

Email inquiries are monitored Monday to Saturday 10am to 5pm

Andie says,

"The Royal Ballet is just amazing and so worth seeing. They perform with a live orchestra."

Dean says,

"The side boxes look fantastic but have a view that's way to the side. I recommend sitting as center as possible so that you can see the entire stage at all times."

No Stair Scare:

There are special dedicated seats for every performance just for those with limited mobility.

Victoria & Albert Museum
[Tantalizing collections await you]

If you think you don't like museums then you haven't seen this one. The V & A is simply astonishing and offers something interesting for everyone in your party. From modern theatre memorabilia to medieval door locks, from costumes by the century to toys of old, this enormous place is the world's greatest museum of design and the arts.

It was inaugurated under its current name in 1899 by Queen Victoria in homage to her beloved, deceased husband, Prince Albert. It's one of the reasons we love London. Don't miss it.

www.vam.ac.uk

Free to enter
There is a nominal fee for their optional special exhibits

Intl. calling: (011) 44-20 7942 2000
Local landline calling: 7942 2000
Local mobile calling: 020 7942 2000

Located on Brompton Road and Cromwell
-in Knightsbridge, London

Open daily to time-reserved visitors
Closed Christmas Eve, Christmas Day, & December 26

Get a Clue:

The V & A has a permanent collection of 4,500,000 items.

Andie says,

"Don't try to see too many sections in one visit. Pick three that interest you and go directly to those floors."

Dean says,

"The grandly arched front entrance has recently been substituted for a new entry point around to the left on Exhibition Road."

Mealtime Clues:

Dine inside this beautiful museum at the V & A Café or at the Garden Café during museum hours. London's famous department store, Harrods is just a five minute walk eastward on Brompton Road and has many cafés and restaurants to choose from.

No Stair Scare:

This museum is fully accessible those with limited mobility.

City Cruises
[A guided tour on the magnificent River Thames]

There's nothing quite like a guided tour where you get to relax on a boat while traversing the city's main waterway. You'll see many camera-worthy views not seen by land, and will learn about all of the interesting sights along the muddy riverbank. It can be a form of transportation as well because you embark at the docks beneath the Tower of London and then disembark at Westminster's Big Ben and Houses of Parliament (or vice-versa.) Hey it's better than being stuck in the London traffic.

www.cityexperiences.com/london/city-cruises

An online ticket reservation is encouraged but not required.

Intl. calling: (011) 44-20 7740 0400
Local calling: 7740 0400
Local mobile calling: 020 7740 0400

Located at Tower Pier, on the River Thames
-in The City, London

* * *

Located at Westminster Pier, on the River Thames
-in Westminster, London

Cruises run everyday, even at Christmastime

Dean says,

"The boats leave every forty minutes so it's pretty easy to catch one."

Cultural Clue:

You can also choose to cruise towards Greenwich, a former royal area in the southeast area of London.

No Stair Scare:

These boats are able to accommodate those with limited mobility.

Harrods
[The grande dame of luxury stores]

Whether you go to purchase or to gawk, Harrods is more than a huge, beautiful store. There are a million reasons to visit it, including its luxury handbags, the latest fashions, sparkling jewelry, and an entire room of different perfumes. We go there for its food halls, which are a work of art unto themselves.

Harrods is the most famous store in London and you need to see it. Admire the Egyptian-styled escalator area as you ascend to one of Harrods many restaurants to enjoy a beautiful lunch. It's the perfect London afternoon.

www.harrods.com

Free to visit

Located at 87 Brompton Road
-in Knightsbridge, London

Intl. calling: (011) 44-20 8479 5100
Local landline calling: 8479 5100
Local mobile calling: 020 8479 5100

Open daily
Closes early on Christmas Eve and New Year's Eve
Closed Christmas Day

Pro Tip:

If you plan on doing some real spending, consider opening a Harrods credit card. If approved, you'll receive 10% off your transaction.

Historical Highlight:

Before its sale in 2010, Harrods was owned by Mohamed Al Fayed, father of Dodi who was killed in the car crash with his lover Diana, Princess of Wales.

No Stair Scare:

All floors are accessible to those with limited mobility.

Mealtime Clue:

There are so many places to eat here that it's actually mind-boggling. From restaurants to food counters to the famous Food Hall, one can never go hungry at Harrods.

West End Shows
[They rival even New York's theatre scene]

London's West End is chock full of old theatre houses and boasts a full range of plays and musicals year round. Many of New York's Broadway shows originate right here. Enjoy a hit by Andrew Lloyd Weber or try something unknown or unusual. The most difficult thing about this will be deciding what to see. Whatever you choose will be great, and probably a highpoint of your visit. Consider seeing the Agatha Christie murder mystery, The Mousetrap. It's London's longest running show and opened in 1952.

Tickets to shows can be purchased ahead of time online at a particular theatre's website (a good idea if it's a current hit that might sell out) or on the same day at London's TKTS theatre ticket booth in Leicester Square or from the TKTS website. The same-day option offers a substantial discount, sometimes even half off, and is a good choice if you don't have your heart set on any specific show.

www.tkts.co.uk

Located in Leicester Square
At the northern end of St. Martin's Lane
-in Soho, London

Tickets: ££-£££
Prices vary by show

Credit & Debit Cards: Yes
Cash: Yes
Accessible: Yes

No telephone contact available for TKTS

Open daily
Closed Christmas Day

Dean says,

"The TKTS Booth has clear signage and is located at the southern edge of Leicester Square. It is a non-profit, trustworthy entity of the London theatre scene. Don't confuse it with the other ticket agent stores and booths in the Square."

Pro Tip:

Note that most of London's shows are dark on Sundays.

Great Clue:

A *What's on Sale* sign at the booth will show that day's offerings and will state how much the discount will be for their special same-day tickets. The shows listed will be separated by matinée and evening performances so make sure you're looking at the one you prefer. Choose two shows in case your first choice is sold out by the time you get to the window.

Andie says,

"In London and in New York, we use TKTS for our show tickets and most of the time the seats are amazing. Sometimes they are VIP seats that were being held aside until the last day."

No Stair Scare:

This ticket booth is welcoming to those with limited mobility.

Nighttime in Shoreditch
[Cocktails as art]

The hippest neighborhood in London is Shoreditch. This area, north of The City, is the hot spot for enigmatic galleries, unusual shops, and an irreverent attitude that's completely irresistible. Don't miss its shining star, Nightjar Speakeasy, a cocktail lounge as quirky as the area. Make a booking well in advance to reserve a table. Their No Standing policy means an uncrowded atmosphere so that you can relax, have fun, and appreciate the wonderful service. Order up tasty tapas or a charcuterie plate to nibble on while you enjoy the best cocktail of your life. Live jazz and old school piano complete the ambiance in this fun, sophisticated, and curious place. We never miss a chance to come here.

Note: Its address here in Shoreditch isn't easy to find, so use Google maps to get near it. Then walk along until your see the red awning of Chicken Cottage and then spy the dark wooden doors with a plaque of a little Nightjar bird. It's between Café Arena and KFC.

Reservations required through their website's live booking system

https://barnightjar.com

Ambience: Hip glamour grunge
Noise level: Medium to loud
Lighting: Dim

Credit Cards: Yes
Accessible: No
WiFi: No

Located at 129 City Road
-in Shoreditch, London

Intl. calling: (011) 44-20 7253 4101
Local landline calling: 7253 4101
Local mobile calling: 020 7253 4101

Open nightly
Closed on some major holidays

Andie says,
"The geniuses at Nightjar completely change their cocktail menu regularly, so you never can know for sure what to expect."

Dean says,
"This is one of those places where planning ahead matters. Their tables are in demand but can be booked up to three months ahead. Pick a date for yourself now and book it!"

Pro Tip:
There are now two Nightjar speakeasies in London. Their newest location is located right in the quaint and very-central tourist area of Carnaby which couldn't be more convenient. It is smaller than the original in Shoreditch but has the same great mixology. (Being the purists that we are, we prefer the one in Shoreditch.) If you can't get a reservation at one then try the other.

Stair Scare:
This venue cannot accommodate those with limited mobility.

Trafalgar Square
[The monumental plaza beckons its citizens]

London's most famous plaza is an impressive sight indeed. Offering a stately gathering place for anyone and everyone, you never know what you'll find going on there. The four giant lion sculptures watch over the ever-changing action while restrained fountains and Lord Nelson atop a tall column complete the visual poetry.

No website

Free public space

Located north of where The Strand meets The Mall
-in Charing Cross, London

Intl. calling: (011) 44-20 7983 4750
Local landline calling: 7983 4750
Local mobile calling: 020 7983 4750

Open 24/7

Historical Highlight:

This public plaza was completed in 1840 in order to commemorate the naval battle known as the Battle of Trafalgar.

Pro Tip:

The large, majestically columned building across from Trafalgar Square is London's National Gallery and holds a prominent collection of paintings. The gorgeous church near it is St. Martins-in-the-Fields, built in 1726.

Cultural Tidbits:

This square is a main gathering place on New Year's Eve, and is graced by a huge Christmas tree given as an annual gift from Norway.

No Stair Scare:

This square is welcoming to those with limited mobility.

Mealtime Clue:

Mother Mash is just a short walk north and offers the tastiest lunch around. (Details in the chapter titled *Feasting*)

Buckingham Palace
[The immense royal residence of King Charles III]

Arguably the most famous building in all of London, one might wonder why Buckingham Palace isn't higher on our *Not to Be Missed* list. The reason is simple... there's not much to do there.

As the official residence of the reigning monarch, visitors are offered entrance for just two months in summer (while His Majesty is on summer holiday) and even then are limited to visits of the staterooms only. Pricy *guided* tours of the staterooms are offered on specific days in late March through April depending on that year's calendar. Aside from those times, all you can do is admire the palace from the outside. The famous changing of the guard does take place on certain days but is really not that interesting. Instead, just take an after-dinner stroll to see it all lit up.

www.royalcollection.org.uk

Located between The Mall and Birdcage Walk, in St. James's Park
-next to St. James's neighborhood, London

Intl. calling: (011) 44-20 7766 7300
Local landline calling: 7766 7300
Local mobile calling: 020 7766 7300

Currently, the Staterooms are open from late July through September, and for limited guided tours in the spring. A reserved ticket time is required and can be secured online or by telephone. This schedule could change under King Charles III.

Historical Highlight:

Queen Victoria was the first monarch to live in Buckingham Palace and took up residence there in 1837. It boasts a whopping seven-hundred and seventy-five rooms.

Dean says,

"The changing of the guard isn't held everyday and is weather dependant. Check the guard's official webpage link below for the most current information."

www.householddivision.org.uk/changing-the-guard

Andie says,

"If you see a food carts near the palace gates, treat yourself... the sausages being sold there are cheap, large, and amazingly delicious! Not at all like an American hotdog."

No Stair Scare:

Both the gardens and the staterooms are fully accessible to those with limited mobility as long as they have a companion caregiver with them. Call them any questions regarding this policy.

A Visit to Windsor Castle
[Residence of Kings and Queens]

Half-day Excursion

If you have a hankering to see a castle— a *real* castle— then you're in luck. Windsor Castle is an easy thirty-five minute train ride from London's Paddington Station and was the regular weekend home of Queen Elizabeth II. It was built during the dark ages in the eleventh century and was expanded and improved upon by nearly every monarch since. Even so, it has never lost its original fortress identity and is glorious both inside and out.

Visitors can explore the grounds, the official dining room, the state apartments, the semi-staterooms, and Queen Mary's immense dollhouse. Admission also includes St. George's Chapel where many impressive royal figures are resting for eternity. All in all, it takes almost two hours to tour it. While you're inside, try to imagine the great hall being used by Edward IV and Queen Elizabeth Woodville all the way back in the 1400's. It's amazing, and definitely worth your time.

www.royalcollection.org.uk/visit/windsorcastle

Reserve a time online for a discounted rate
-Also available by telephone

Located on the hillside,
-in the Town of Windsor
Berkshire County, England

Intl. calling: (011) 44 303 123 7304
Local mobile calling: 0303 123 7304

Open to visitors on most days; check their calendar
Closed on Tuesdays and Wednesdays, and some major holidays

Pro Tip:

To make the most of your visit here, use their website to choose a day when both the St. Georges Chapel *and* the state apartments are open. We mention this because there are days throughout the year when one or the other are closed for special functions. The incredibly important chapel is open on Mondays, Thursdays, Fridays, and Saturdays. We mention this because it is a major part of a visit to Windsor Castle!

Historical Highlight:

The castle was built by William the Conqueror, the same king who built the Tower of London (another royal residence.) A section of the castle had to be restored after a large fire in 1992.

Dean says,

"Inside St. Georges Chapel you can visit the tombs of many famous people, including Henry VIII and Jane Seymour, Edward IV and Elizabeth Woodville, Charles I, and even the Queen Mother of QEII (and grandmother of King Charles III.) Many of Queen Victoria's children were married in the chapel, as were Harry and Meghan."

Andie says,

"Inside the room which displays the elaborate dollhouse of Queen Mary, there's a lovely presentation of gifts from the French government to George VI for his daughters. They are all designer clothing pieces *for dolls* but were made by Worth, Lanvin, Cartier, Hermès and Vuitton."

Loo Clue:

When you exit the castle after touring it you'll find yourself in an outdoor courtyard with a gift shop to one side and some benches for seating. If you need toilette facilities (of which there are none inside for public use) walk past the benches and take a right. Follow along the outside of the castle until you come upon the modern men's and women's lavatories which have been built especially for visitors to the castle.

No Stair Scare:

The castle is up a steep hill but is fully accessible to those with limited mobility (with assistance from the staff there.) You might even get to ride in The King's personal elevator.

Candy Alert:

The town of Windsor is charming, and one of our favorite English treats, the Fudge Kitchen, has a shop there. They make handmade fudge in gourmet flavors that will blow your mind. Pick some up while you're here.

* * *

By train: Central London to Windsor Castle

Take a train from London to Windsor, which requires a very easy change of trains (on the same platform) at Slough. Everyone getting off there will be doing the same thing so just follow the pack. Here are the simple instructions:

- Inside Paddington Station, go to a ticket window or Trainline ticket machine and purchase round trip 1st or 2nd class tickets to **Windsor & Eton Central.** Windsor-bound 2nd class seats cost around £10 each way on most days and run frequently, sometimes as often as every twenty minutes. Tickets may be purchased ahead of time online and then claimed at a Trainline machine. Visit this special link:

   www.thetrainline.com/stations/windsor-eton-riverside

- Board a train carriage (marked on the outside with a 1 for first class or a 2 for second class) and find your seats. Present your tickets to the conductor when he comes by, and be sure to **take the ticket with you when you disembark**. You may have to show it in order to exit your arrivals station!

- At Slough, wait on the platform for the next train heading for Windsor. This will usually be just a few minutes. *You'll only be on the Slough train for one stop.*

- Exit the Windsor & Eton Central station and walk five minutes uphill to the castle. Trust us; you'll know it when you see it.

To return to London, just stroll back to the Windsor & Eton rail station and wait on the platform for your train. *Simply do the same trip in reverse, once again disembarking with your used tickets intact in case they're required for exit at Paddington Station in London.*

A Visit to Hampton Court Palace
[Welcome to the world of Henry VIII]

Half-day Excursion

Need another reason to get out of town for awhile? Tudor finery at its best awaits you at this royal retreat in greater London. Walk the very halls and throne rooms of Henry VIII and admire his breathtaking Great Hall where he first danced with the infamous Anne Boleyn. Their courtship changed the path of English history and religion forever. Visitors are graciously allowed entrance to the exquisite chapel where Henry married several of his wives including Boleyn. The palace's complimentary audio guides will enhance your visit with insightful glimpses into the past. Take advantage of them.

There's always a lot to see at Hampton Court Palace and an average visit can easily last three hours. Experience the oldest, best-preserved kitchens in Britain, quadrupled in size by orders of King Henry himself. Then explore the magic garden or outwit your loved ones in the hedge maze.

www.hrp.org.uk/hampton-court-palace

Tickets are limited!
Pre-book your reservation online or by phone to avoid disappointment

Located thirty minutes west of central London,
-on the River Thames in East Moseley, Surry

Intl. calling: (011) 44-20 3166 6000
Local landline calling: 3166-6000
Local mobile calling 020 3166 6000

Seasonal opening hours
Check their online calendar for your dates
Closed on Christmas Eve, Christmas Day, & Dec. 26

Historical Highlight:

Hampton Court was a grand palace built by Cardinal Thomas Wolsey beginning in 1514 and at the time of its completion was thought to be the greatest palace ever built. But it's never smart to have a palace grander and more opulent then The King's and so when Wolsey fell out of favor with Henry VIII, Hampton Court got a new resident.

It had to be enlarged to hold the royal court, which was done in short order, and then later was enlarged again, and modernized in style, by the prominent architect Christopher Wren in 1689. Only part of this modernization was completed however, causing today's palace to have two distinctly different styles, the old Tudor next to the newer Stuart. You'll see and appreciate both sections during your visit there.

Pro Tip:

This is a lively place and there's always something special going on, from historical cooking demonstrations and chocolate making in the old kitchens, to art exhibits, garden talks, jousting tournaments, and a children's Magic Garden complete with a dragon. On several nights in June and July, world class singers offer concerts right on the palace grounds. Check their online calendar for updates.

Dean says,

"The easiest and fastest way for both Henry VIII and Elizabeth I to travel between Hampton Court and London was by boat on the Thames."

Andie says,

"High above, inside the Great Hall, notice the colorful carved figures peering down at you from the eaves. They were placed there as a cautionary reminder to the courtiers that nothing in the Great Hall was unseen or unheard, and are the original source of the word eavesdropper."

Some Stair Scare:

A majority of this palace is accessible to those with limited mobility.

Mealtime Clue:

You're welcome to bring your own food and have a picnic in their park. Visit a Paul bakery before you depart on the London train; they have everything you need for a great picnic lunch. (Details in the chapter titled Treats) The palace also has picnic items and beverages for sale.

Transportation Clues:

Getting to the palace is easy. The South West Trains take only thirty-five minutes to make the nine stops to Hampton Court from London's Waterloo Station, which is located on the Thames' south riverbank near the London Eye. Trains run every half hour. (This is also how you get to Wimbledon.) For detailed train information, visit Southwest Trains online.

Note: Stations abbreviations are: WAT to HMC. Specify that a return trip is needed. (If you're using a London transportation pay-as-you-go Oyster Card, it will be accepted as payment - Zone 6.)

PART 2
[Try to Fit it in]

RIB speed boats are more thrilling than you can imagine

Thames RIB Experience
[Don't knock it until you've tried it]

Our decision to include jet boats speeding down the River Thames within this first chapter might surprise some readers, but it really shouldn't. We like to have fun and this experience is off the charts. In fact, it's unforgettable.

There's no way to describe the thrill you get when your super-fast Rigid Inflatable Boat veers into a sharp turn so you'll just have to trust us. You'll be laughing harder than you have laughed in a long time. All of this craziness happens in a quieter section of river; on your way there you get to enjoy some music and a live narrative of things along the riverbank that you've always wondered about but never knew. The crew is top notch and will take good care of you.

There are no seatbelts because you'll be wearing a life-preserver vest. And no, you will not get wet. Try to book it in advance with an eye on the weather forecast. It often sells out!

https://thamesribexperience.com

An online reservation and ticket is strongly encouraged

Usually disembarks from Embankment Pier (check your booking to verify)
-On the water dock in front of the Charing Cross Tube station
Just off the Strand, London

Intl. calling: (011) 44 20 3245 1177
Local landline calling: 3245 1177
Local mobile calling: 020 3245 1177

Speeding on the river everyday

Pro Tip:

You must be a certain height to enjoy this ride so some children may not be allowed. Their guidelines are on the website.

Dean says,

"There are different experiences to choose from. Book the *Canary Wharf Experience*."

A little Stair Scare:

This experience is available to those with limited mobility as long as they are accompanied by a caregiver that can assist in boarding.

The National Gallery
[Britain's finest collection of paintings]

Unlike New York, London boasts a museum just for paintings. The National Gallery houses Britain's world class collection, all of which could be considered national treasures. This immense gallery, which seems an insufficient word for so large a place, is located facing Trafalgar Square. Its grand, columned portico creates a lovely backdrop to the famous plaza. Inside, visitors will find a vast collection including such famous paintings as:

Botticelli's Mars and Venus
Delaroche's The Execution of Lady Jane Grey
Rembrandt's Self Portrait
van Gogh's Sunflowers
da Vinci's Virgin of the Rocks
Vermeer's Lady Standing at a Virginal

There's a rare, unfinished painting by Michelangelo, and major works by Titian, Degas, Manet, Monet, Seurat, and others creating a mind-boggling assortment which may make you feel as if all masterpieces live there.

With such human achievement at hand you might wonder why we didn't place the National Gallery in our Not To Be Missed section. Here's why: it's overwhelming. Its sprawling maze of rooms used to be difficult to navigate and had no natural flow for the visitor; this has improved since the pandemic forced the museum to create three one-way routes for viewing the art. Even if you know which room a particular painting is in, you'll still need patience finding it. The three designated routes should be in effect for some time.

The affect on the visitor from too much art will obviously add to the probability of them coming down with a bad case of hyperkulturemia. We recommend going to this museum first thing in the morning while you're still rested and fresh. It's free, so give it a go.

www.nationalgallery.org.uk

Free to enter
An online ticket can be reserved ahead to save time; their in-person ticket queue can get quite long.

Located at Trafalgar Square
-in Westminster, London

Intl. calling: (011) 44 20 7747 2885
Local landline calling: 7747 2885
Local mobile calling: 020 7747 2885

Open daily to visitors with reservations
Closed on New Year's Day, Christmas Eve, Christmas Day, and December 26

Pro Tip:

Add insight to your visit by choosing a specialized Audio Guide Tour, available for a nominal fee from one of the Audio Guide desks on level two.

Dean says,

"The National Gallery has some 2,300 paintings. Its sister-museum, the National Portrait Gallery, is incredible and one of our favorite sights in London. Unfortunately it is currently closed for renovation until late June of 2023."

Some Stair Scare:

This museum is partially accessible to those with limited mobility.

Mealtime Clue:

If you feel peckish between paintings, don't worry. There are several places to get something to eat including the National Dining Rooms, the National Café, or their lovely espresso bar.

Dennis Severs House
[A London townhouse transformed into the past]

This is exactly the kind of unique, fascinating place that we love to discover and then include in our travel books. It is simply explained but not simply understood...

In the 1970's a man named Dennis Severs bought a property in the Spitalfields area of London and over time filled it top to bottom with his passion: items from past centuries that he had fondly collected. Today visitors to his house can experience it a very unusual way. The house is open to guests with a reservation and while it is open during the day, we recommend a nighttime visit.

A silent walk-through of this house is nothing less than a surreal experience. There will be moments when you feel as if you have gone back in time. Everything inside is arranged as if the family who lives there is nearby –perhaps just in the next room. You can occasionally hear them, and their dinner is still on the table as if they were suddenly interrupted. Candles and fireplaces throughout are lit and yet you seem to be the only one there. Does that make you a ghost? An intruder? It's hard to say.

Call it a living museum; call it a historic experience. It is difficult to define this unusual sight but it's completely delightful to visit. Other sensory experiences are part of it as well, like scents and sounds, which makes it all the more mysterious and wonderful. As Mr. Severs himself used to say, *You either see it or you don't.* We see it.

https://dennissevershouse.co.uk

An online booking is usually required

Located at 18 Folgate Street
-in Spitalfields, London

Intl. calling: (011) 44-20 7247 4013
Local landline calling: 7247 4013
Local mobile calling: 020 7247 4013

Open Thursday through Sunday to visitors with reservations
With expanded days during the Christmas holiday period

Pro Tip:

Book your preferred time weeks in advance.

Andie says,

"I love that even the sense of smell is involved here. Candles, perfume, the fireplaces, even the food on the table. It truly is an amazing experience."

Dean says,

"This is my new favorite thing in London."

Stair Scare:

This house museum has old stairways and therefore is not accessible to those with limited mobility.

Mealtime Clue:

There are a ton of restaurants in and around the famous Spitalfields Market nearby.

British Museum
[The other collections, curious and uncommon]

This museum exhibits the country's non-painting treasures; it quite literally has everything else. Housed in an immense classically-styled structure which grew even larger with the addition of several wings, the British Museum is now a formidable place. For those who love objects from the ancient world, this is your museum. Don't miss the Rosetta Stone... it was this inscribed chunk of rock that made translating Egyptian hieroglyphics possible. One warning: you have to really like museums to enjoy this place.

www.britishmuseum.org

Free to enter
An online reservation time is encouraged, but walk-up entry is possible.
Nominal fee for some optional special exhibits

Located at Bloomsbury Street and Great Russell Street
-in Bloomsbury, London

Intl. calling: (011) 44-20 7323 8299
Local landline calling: 7323 8299
Local mobile calling: 020 7323 8299

Open daily to visitors with reservations
Closed on Good Friday, Christmas Eve, Christmas Day, December 26, and New Year's Day

Pro Tip:

The best time of day to visit this highly popular museum and avoid the crowds is on weekdays from 10am to 11am.

Andie says,

"Famous for having nearly all of the statues and carved reliefs from the Parthenon in Athens, visitors now view a sign apologizing that the wing housing them is closed for the time being. This includes the fabulous Elgin Marbles. It seems that Greece might want them returned."

Dean says,

"The Great Court that sits in the center of the museum is truly breathtaking."

A Little Stair Scare:

This museum is largely accessible to those with limited mobility. Entry is from the self-operable lifts by the steps on Great Russell Street, at their south entrance.

Mealtime Clue:

Plenty of food options await you at the museum. Varied menus can be found at their Court Café or Pizzeria. Or opt for the Great Court Restaurant and dine under the amazing atrium ceiling. Afternoon Tea is served daily as well as a full menu.

Tate Modern
[London's quirky and wonderful art museum]

The Tate Modern is Britain's national gallery of international art dating from 1900 to the present. This fun and unusual place has been delighting visitors since 2000 and even has an interactive digital drawing bar on level one where you can create a design that instantly becomes displayed on the museum's virtual mosaic.

Permanent collections include works by such esteemed artists as Dali, Picasso, Lichtenstein, Hockney, and Matisse. If you're a lover of modern art then you simply can't miss this place. And it's all there for free!

www.tate.org.uk/visit/tate-modern

Free to enter, no reservation needed
There is a nominal fee for their optional special exhibits

Located on the bankside of Millennium Bridge
-in Southbank, London
South of the River Thames

Intl. calling: (011) 44-20 7887 8888
Local landline calling: 7887 8888
Local mobile calling: 020 7887 8888

Open daily to visitors with reservations
Closed on Christmas Eve, Christmas Day, and Dec. 26

Mealtime Clue:

London's thousand-year-old food festival, *Borough Market* offers many restaurants and snacking opportunities and is about a seven minute walk east from the Tate Modern.

Cultural Clue:

Shakespeare's Globe Theatre is right next door, along the riverbank.

No Stair Scare:

This museum is accommodating to those with limited mobility.

Natural History Museum
[Dinosaurs and other creatures in a gorgeous building]

The giant stone structure right next door to the Victoria and Albert Museum just happens to be a visual spectacle inside and out. It's London's natural history museum and the building interior alone is worth a visit (which is free, by the way) and your kids will love the dinosaurs. It's definitely the fanciest natural history museum we've ever seen. If you don't have a time reservation to enter, don't fret. Ask the ticket-checker at the front if you can go on inside because it's usually not a problem, especially on a weekday.

www.nhm.ac.uk

Free to enter
-An online reservation is recommended to avoid disappointment
There is a nominal fee for any optional special exhibits

Located at Cromwell Road and Exhibition Road
-in Knightsbridge, London

Intl. calling: (011) 44-20 7942 5000
Local landline calling: 7942 5000
Local mobile calling: 020 7942 5000

Open daily
Closed on Christmas Eve, Christmas Day, and Dec. 26

Mealtime Clue:

This museum boasts several good eateries including one called The Kitchen. It serves up fresh sandwiches, desserts, and various beverages so that you and your loved one can refuel.

Pro Tip:

Don't try to see this museum on the same day as the V & A Museum next door. You will be forced to do too much walking and there's just too much for your brain to take in!

No Stair Scare:

This museum is accommodating to those with limited mobility. Both of its main entrances are step free.

The London Eye
[The ultimate observation deck]

An ever-changing view from a seat in a glass and steel capsule is a thrilling thing, no question about it. This is what you get at the London Eye, a kind of mutant Ferris wheel that rises high above the nearby skyline. The slow, graceful rotation lasts a full thirty minutes. Share this unique experience with a loved one for a romantic moment and get your camera ready for some great shots.

www.londoneye.com

A timed reservation made on their website will guarantee you entry and a discount.
Walk-up entry is possible at their ticket queue.

Located on the south riverbank
-in Lambeth, London
Near Westminster Bridge

Intl. calling: (011) 44-871 781 3000
Local landline calling: 871 781 3000

Open daily
Closed on Christmas Day

Party Clue:

A private capsule (with or without champagne and nibbles) for you and your friends is available starting at around £600. It includes queue-less VIP boarding.

Andie says,

"If you're afraid of heights or dislike enclosed spaces, you may want to pass on this one."

Dean says,

"This attraction is so popular that during the high season it can take in an average of £20,000 an hour."

No Stair Scare:

This attraction is fully accessible to those with limited mobility.

Piccadilly Circus and Jermyn Street
[Centerpiece of humanity and shopping]

One can't visit London without taking in the sights and sounds of Piccadilly Circus and Jermyn Street (which runs south of the Piccadilly plaza.) You'll probably find yourself smack dab on the middle of this famous area at some point anyway. It's easily recognized by the winged statue on the top of the Shaftesbury Memorial Fountain, or by its bright collection of huge neon billboards.

Connecting Regent Street to other streets just east of the traffic circle, Piccadilly Circus always seems like the center of everything. Stop and people-watch for awhile, or window shop on Jermyn Street for that special souvenir.

No website

Free public plaza and shopping street

Located at the junction of Regent and Piccadilly St.
-in Westminster, London

No general telephone contact

Shops in this area have varied hours of operation.

Great Clue:

One of London's largest Underground train stations is right in the circus.

Dean says,

"Don't miss a chance to visit the amazing Paxton & Whitfield cheese shop on Jermyn Street."

No Stair Scare:

This area is welcoming to those with limited mobility.

Mealtime Clues:

You simply can't be this close to Mother Mash and not have lunch there. Go now, and don't forget to order bangers with Farmer's Gravy. (Details in the chapter titled Feasting)

For dinner, Veeraswamy is located right on gorgeous Regent Street and was London's very first Indian restaurant. For an elegant meal, call for a table at (011) 44-20 7734 1401.

Andie says:

"Children are welcome at Veeraswamy but only until 8pm. After that, the dining room is for adults only."

Shakespeare's Globe Theatre
[A modern day replica]

One of the most enduring things coming out of England's Elizabethan era was the work of one William Shakespeare. The round, open-air theatre that sat *almost* on this spot in the early 1600's was built by his theatre company and featured his plays. That old Globe Theatre eventually burnt to the ground but in 1997 an oak and thatched replica of the original was recreated here. It features classically-trained actors in live performances from May through October.

A secondary replica set indoors is of the old Blackfriar's Theatre and is also part of this complex. Tickets to either should be purchased ahead of time online or by telephone. If there are no performances offered during your visit to London then consider taking a guided tour of the place. It's very informative and gives you an intimate look at the entire venue.

www.shakespearesglobe.com

Regarding the guided tours:

Their one hour tours need to be booked ahead online or by phone

Located at 21 New Globe Walk
-in Bankside, London (South of the River Thames)

Curtain Clue:
At performance time, the floor section called *The Yard* is standing only. The circular balconies do offer seating but consist of a backless bench with cushions. This is authentic to the original Elizabethan design.

Intl. calling: (011) 44-20 7902 1500
Local landline calling: 7902 1500
Local mobile calling: 020 7902 1500

See their online tour calendar for available days.
No tours on Christmas Eve or Christmas Day

Dean says,

"This is a working theatre so check out all of their upcoming performances."

Andie says,

"I adore the little Sam Wanamaker Playhouse. You really feel as if you have gone back in time to the old *Blackfriar's Theatre* where Shakespeare's plays were also performed."

Historical Highlight:

The original Globe theatre was built in 1599 and sat about 750' away from this new one. It was a bit larger and certainly not as safe, packing in 3,000 spectators instead of today's 1,400.

No Stair Scare:

This theatre is accessible to those with limited mobility.

A Train to Bath, England
[Thermal waters beckon visitors since Roman times]

Full-day Excursion

Thanks to some very talented architects in the 1700's, Bath is beautiful. Astoundingly beautiful. The entire town is a protected UNESCO World Heritage Site which should tell you something right there. It's located in Somerset County, a western section of the English countryside. Its hotels are quaint and more affordable than comparable ones in London and a night or two in Bath definitely has its charms. But this is one place that also works fine as a day trip as long as you visit for the *entire* day.

When conquering Romans heard about hot thermal waters flowing up from the ground in this area of England they went to work building a sacred but usable bath complex on the spot. This phenomenon was considered a gift from the gods and curative for many ailments and diseases. The town around it slowly grew and today is still known as *Bath.* Popular interest in curative waters during England's Georgian period made the place a hot spot, so to speak, and it seems everyone who was anyone went there. This caused great development which included the building of the cathedral-like Bath Abbey, a social center called the Pump Room where one could sip a glass of the thermal waters, the beautiful Pulteney Bridge, and sections of fine apartments for the well-heeled. Its society included the famous author Jane Austen who featured Bath in two of her novels. Even Charles Dickens had his characters "taking the waters" there.

In our opinion there are three things you simply must do while in Bath. First, tour the original Roman baths from 60 AD (restored by Victorian architects) then "take the waters" yourself in the gorgeous new Thermae Spa complex, and finish the day with an elegant and relaxing Afternoon Tea service at the Royal Crescent. If you have time, peek inside the Bath Abbey as well.

Trains run direct from London's Paddington Station and bring you right into the center of town. Leave early and don't forget to pack your swimwear.

Tour of the ancient Roman Baths

www.romanbaths.co.uk

A reservation and timed-ticket are now required
(Book online or by telephone)

Located in the Abbey Churchyard
-in Bath, Somerset, England

Intl. calling: (011) 44 1225 477785
Local landline calling: 1225 477785

Open daily in high season; limited hours begin in September.
Closed Christmas Day

Pro Tip:
The ruins are fascinating, but don't dally there too long inside or you won't have time to explore the rest of Bath.

Mealtime Clue:

As you exit the Roman Baths you'll find yourself right inside the dining room of the Pump Room. This lovely Georgian gathering place houses the actual pump of warm mineral water that has been savored by many health-seekers in the last three-hundred years, and the dining room offers a varied menu. For die-hard Jane Austen fans, this will be a pinch-me moment.

Some Stair Scare:

There are some definite obstacles in this historic site when it comes to being visited by someone with limited mobility. Check their website though because on certain days at 10am and then again at 3pm, they turn the entire place in to an accessible layout for everybody.

Treat Alert:

Don't miss the Fudge Kitchen, conveniently located right across from the entrance to the ancient Roman Baths. Handmade and quite gourmet!

* * *

Spa visit to the modern Thermae Bath

www.thermaebathspa.com

No one under age sixteen admitted
Basic admission includes a two-hour visit to the indoor & outdoor thermal pools, aroma steam rooms, waterfall shower, towel, bathrobe, slippers and café entrance.

-Many additional spa services available a la carte

Pre-booked sessions purchased by telephone or online are now required

Intl. calling: (011) 44 1225 33 1234
Local landline calling: 1225 33 1234

Located on Hot Bath Street
(Duh, where else would it be?)
-in Bath, Somerset, England

Open to visitors with pre-booked reservations
Limited hours may be offered in the low season so check their online calendar.
Closed Christmas Day, Dec. 26, and New Year's Day

Pro Tip:

The modern spa is readily available Monday through Thursday but can have a long queue on the weekends. Plan ahead and book your time slot.

Andie says,

"The indoor pool has massage jets, a whirlpool, and even a lazy river. The natural temperature of the water is 92 degrees."

No Stair Scare:

The thermal baths complex is fully accessible to those with limited mobility.

* * *

Afternoon Tea at the Royal Crescent

Pulteney Bridge, Bath Abbey, the Circus, and the Royal Crescent are four of the most astonishing works of architecture in Bath. Since you'll want to give the Royal Crescent a look, why not reserve a table for Afternoon Tea there? (While there are many places to have tea in this tiny town, the Royal Crescent Hotel offers the most sumptuous and delicious one.) And it's inexpensive when compared to Afternoon Tea in London!

Reservations strongly recommended

www.royalcrescent.co.uk/afternoon-tea

Located at 16 Royal Crescent
-in Bath, Somerset, England

Intl. Calling: (011) 44 1225 823 333
Local landline calling: 1225 823 333

Dean says,
"The cream-colored material used to create the buildings of this unique town is called Bath Stone and is a local resource. There's also a locally-made blue glass called Bath Glass, and a shop near the Roman Baths offers a wide assortment to purchase."

No Stair Scare:
This venue is accommodating to those with limited mobility.

Transportation Details

By train: Central London to Bath Spa

Take a direct train to Bath and avoid the hassle *and* the traffic. Compared to a bus from Victoria Station, the train cuts the travel time in half but is the more expensive option. Since we hate to waste time, we consider this a worthwhile splurge. Here are the simple instructions:

- Inside Paddington Station, go to a ticket window or Trainline ticket machine and purchase round trip 1st or 2nd class tickets to **Bath Spa.** 2nd class seats cost £25 to £44 each way depending on the day of the week. Trains run frequently, sometimes as often as every half hour. Tickets may be purchased ahead online and then claimed at a Trainline machine. Visit their website at: **www.thetrainline.com/train-times/london-paddington-to-bath-spa**

- Board a train carriage (marked on the outside with a 1 for first class or a 2 for second class) and find your seats. Present your tickets to the conductor when he comes by, and be sure to **take the tickets with you when you disembark**. You'll have to show them in order to exit Bath Station!

- After approximately ninety minutes or so you'll disembark at Bath Station. To get your bearings, stroll a few blocks north to Terrace Walk which is considered the center of town.

Return to London: Walk back to Bath Station and head for the correct platform. It's best to arrive at least fifteen minutes before your scheduled train as it can get crowded. *Save your used tickets in case they're asked for at your Paddington station arrival.*

Dean says,

"We do not recommend a "Bath bus tour" from London. It's highly touted, but is eleven hours long with most of it *spent on the bus*. These buses get stuck in traffic, and only visit the Roman Baths with a short drive-around afterward. The tours *sound* great because they usually include a quick stop at Windsor Castle and Stonehenge on the way. But both Windsor and Bath are more enjoyable when done on your own, and Stonehenge is pointless because people are no longer allowed to get near the ancient stone circle and must view it from some distance away."

Andie says,

"From London, the train is the only realistic way to get to and from Bath. Even the 'direct buses' make a day trip to Bath impossible. Just too slow."

PART 3

[Skip it Unless it's Your Thing]

Queen Victoria still reigns in front of Kensington Palace where she grew up

Kensington Palace & Hyde Park
[Swans and a palace make for the perfect picnic]

Normally, we adore palaces and urge our readers to visit them. In the case of Kensington Palace, we urge you more to the gorgeous surroundings that it enjoys. We're speaking about Hyde Park of course, specifically the Kensington Gardens section. When you're there you can just imagine young Victoria running after her dog, Dash through its lush environs. The famous Round Pond is nearby and lives up to its reputation as a bird sanctuary; the swans that call it home are simply amazing and quite friendly. All of this makes for a storybook experience to be sure –not so much inside the palace itself. Let us explain…

Visitors can buy a ticket (online or in person) and then line up at the entrance opposite the pond. Once inside, you're welcome to follow a one-way walk around which features the rooms where little Victoria lived, as well as another wing where the Georgian Kings and Queens held audience. Unfortunately, Victoria's rooms are not visually exciting and have somewhat contrived props in them (some real form the period, some not.)

Signage is good here so there is no need to book a special tour with a guide; save your money because everyone goes along the same path and sees the same thing. We recommend skipping the tour in favor of having a picnic on the grounds instead. If the weather is fine you won't find a prettier picnic spot in all of London.

www.hrp.org.uk/kensington-palace

Book ahead online, or buy your entry tickets in-person.

Located at Kensington Gardens Marylebone Road
-on the east side of Hyde Park

Intl. calling: (011) 44-333 320 6000
Local landline calling: 333 320 6000

Open Wednesday through Sunday
Closed Mondays and Tuesdays from November through April
Usually open daily in the warmer months
Closed on Christmas Eve, Christmas Day, and Dec. 26

Dean says,

"The palace is still a family home so that is why you only get to tour a small, historic portion of it. It is currently the London home of William and Kate whenever they are in town."

Historical Highlight:

"This is the location where actress Meghan Markle lived with Prince Harry during their engagement."

No Stair Scare:

The palace is accessible to those with limited mobility.

Madame Tussauds Wax Museum
[Tourist groups descend on this London original]

Generally speaking, we're not ones to visit a wax museum and have not endorsed any in our other travel books. This one is the exception because it's the original.

First opened in 1836 as a modest exhibition of wax sculptures by a Frenchwoman named Marie Tussaud, this London gallery has now grown into a veritable theme park. Basic admission features up-close and personal viewing of hundreds of celebrity and historical wax replicas which are precise to the height, size, and features of the actual person they depict. Entry to an elaborate Star Wars experience and Marvel 4D movie are also included. (Their display of Princess Leia with Jabba the Hutt is so realistic and spot-on that it makes you do a double-take!)

If you don't mind crowds, are in a silly mood, have bored children, or are a child at heart yourself, then go and have a fun time at Madame Tussauds. But if you have even an inkling that this is just not your thing, stay away because it probably isn't.

www.madametussauds.com/london

Pre-book your tickets online and receive a discount. In-person entry is available as well at their ticket queue.

Located on Marylebone Road
-in Marylebone, London
Near the Baker Street Underground Station

Intl. calling: (011) 44-871 894 3000
Local landline calling: 871 894 3000

Open daily
Closed on Christmas Day

Dean says,

"Taking photos with the wax sculptures is allowed so have fun with it. The figures look totally real in photos."

Andie says,

"The *Sherlock Holmes Experience* is the museum's newest attraction and features a live, theatrical walk-through that challenges guests to use clues to solve a mystery."

Pro Tip:

The queues at this tourist attraction are infamous but the recent addition of reserved time slots has helped a lot. If money isn't an issue then consider paying a premium rate for the priority entrance ticket or for the VIP entry.

Great Clues:

There are no lockers, so don't arrive with anything you're not prepared to carry throughout the attraction.

Historical Highlight:

Their Chamber of Horrors was a feature of the first Madame Tussauds in 1836 and was an instant hit. It featured gruesome items from the French Revolution. It's currently closed with no plan to reopen.

No Stair Scare:

This venue is accessible to those with limited mobility. Call ahead to let them know what day you are coming, in case they need to assist you in any way.

London Big Bus Tours
[A guided city-tour atop a double-decker bus]

Feel the summer breeze in your hair as you're seated on the open top of a big, red, double-decker bus. It's fun, and the photo ops are endless. You get to see many of London's neighborhoods all in one day and can hop off if there's something you want to explore further. Stop to have an impromptu lunch... another Big Bus will come by every ten to twenty minutes and they're all at your disposal.

www.bigbustours.com/en/london/london-bus-tours

Pre-book tickets online for big savings compared to the sidewalk price!

Buses can be boarded at any of their stops, including:
Baker Street Station, Marble Arch, Trafalgar Square, Green Park and Victoria Station

Intl. calling: (011) 44-20 7808 6753
Local landline calling: 7808 6753
Local mobile calling: 020 7808 6753

Buses run daily
Closed on Christmas Day

Great Clue:
   This type of tour is highly affected by traffic patterns and is best used as a tour. We don't recommend the Big Bus as a method of transportation to get around town.

Pro Tip:

The Red Tour is hop-on/hop-off and can be boarded at any of the stops. It's full circuit, and takes approximately two hours with live commentary.

Dean says,

"If you book online for an open date e-ticket, you will receive a discount and the info will be sent right to your smart phone so you're ready to ride anytime. This makes it very convenient."

Andie says,

"While indoor and outdoor seating are both offered, we endorse the outdoor (upstairs) seating making this tour something you should only do on a fair weather day. It's just not the same from the lower deck."

Great Clue:

The buses all have free WiFi.

No Stair Scare:

These buses are accommodating to those with limited mobility.

Big Ben and the Houses of Parliament
[Tour parliament or enjoy its gorgeous exterior]

Walk in the footsteps of Britain's monarchs and governmental greats as you take in some fascinating history at London's parliament building. Visitors are welcomed in by way of a multi-language audio guide tour that lasts around an hour or so. Eleven rooms are included in this walk-around, and feature Westminster Hall, the Norman Porch, The King's Robing Room, the Royal Gallery, the Prince's Chamber, and others.

Officially called the Palace of Westminster, this glorious neo-Gothic masterpiece was built around a pre-existing royal palace from 1025 AD. The old palace was used by all monarchs up until 1547 when Edward VI, son of Henry VIII, decided it was too old for his taste and went to live elsewhere. He granted the palace to his parliament where it has held its sessions ever since. After a devastating fire in 1834, most of the palace had to be rebuilt. This is when it took on the neo-Gothic look we see today.

The palace's newly restored clock tower fondly known as Big Ben was renamed the "Elizabeth Tower" in 2012 to honor QEII. This tower structure with its huge chiming clock was added in 1859 and now once again keeps perfect time. It is bright and shiny again and even has its numbers and clock-hands in their original blue color. The tower itself cannot actually be visited by the public but is glorious when viewed and photographed from the exterior, especially since the completion of the five-year restoration.

www.parliament.uk/visiting

A pre-booked, timed tour reservation is encouraged to avoid disappointment. Spots are very limited.

Located on the riverbank
-in Westminster, London
Visitor entrance is at 3 St. Margaret's Street

Intl. calling: (011) 44-20 7219 4114
Local landline calling: 7219 4114
Local mobile calling: 020 7219 4114
Telephones are monitored Monday to Saturday from 9am to 5pm

Open most days
Check their online calendar for *your* dates

Family Clue:

Audio guides are available in a family version which has been made more entertaining and understandable for children.

Historical Highlight:

The rebuilt palace that we see today has eleven-hundred rooms.

Mealtime Clue:

An afternoon tea with a window view of the River Thames is offered on tour days. Book this experience ahead, if desired.

Andie says,

"If you can't visit on a day when the tours are running, don't despair. You can still have a peek inside by visiting the Public Gallery."

Dean says,

"The nickname *Big Ben* actually refers to the heaviest bell inside the clock. It has five bells total."

No Stair Scare:

The Houses of Parliament are accessible to those with limited mobility.

St. Paul's Cathedral
[Enjoy an Evensong inside Wren's masterpiece]

Ah! St. Paul's, where Lady Diana Spencer married Charles, Prince of Wales. For this reason alone, a visit here might be at the top of your list... it's not however on the top of ours. This architectural achievement by Sir Christopher Wren begun in 1675 is visually pleasing both inside and out but simply not worth the inexplicable high entry fee just to take a look around.

That said, it should be noted that their *evensong* concerts are free to all who attend and a good way to get inside, and with musical accompaniment. The nightly performances add much to the stiff surroundings so note the times below.

www.stpauls.co.uk

Book an online, timed ticket to avoid disappoint.
In-person ticket purchasing is often possible but not guaranteed.

Religious services and all Evensong concerts are free
The Evensong concerts are held Monday to Saturday at 5pm and on Sundays at 3pm.

Located at St. Paul's Churchyard
-just north of the Millennium Bridge, London

Intl. calling: (011) 44-20 7246 8350
Local landline calling: 7246 8350
Local mobile calling: 020 7246 8350

Open to visitors with a reservation
Sundays are for religious services only
Check their online calendar for exceptions, services, concerts, and special holiday hours

Pro Tip:

You can purchase tickets online for the same day if there are slots still available.

Dean says,

"Although St. Paul's is in the same neighborhood as our *Historic Pub Crawl*, we don't recommend combining the two on the same afternoon!"

No Stair Scare:

The church is accessible to those with limited mobility. The visitor and one companion will both receive free entry but still need to reserve a time slot through the website above.

Chinatown
[Frenetic restaurants in a colorful neighborhood]

Chinatown is one of London's most famous neighborhoods. Situated around the pedestrian-only Gerard Street in an area between Covent Garden and Piccadilly Circus, this colorful section of town is seemingly as popular as ever. Sectioned off by red lanterns and moon gates, it's now the largest (and most centrally-located) Chinatown in the UK and Europe. Go there if you want a well priced, authentic Asian meal or Chinese bakery item. No reservations necessary; just walk around until you find a place you like the look of and give it a try. For us, the food is a bit too authentic!

No website

Free public area

Located at Wardour Street & Lisle Street
-in the West End, London
Just north of Leicester Square

Intl. calling: (011) 44-20 7333 8118
Local landline calling: 7333 8118
Local mobile calling: 020 7333 8118
General information only

Most shops and eateries here are open daily

No Stair Scare:

This area is welcoming to those with limited mobility.

Mealtime Clue:

Go to Opium if you like an exotic cocktail with your lobster dumplings. Reservations are suggested: **http://opiumchinatown.com**

Andie says,

For truly memorable Asian cuisine in London, hurry over to Red Farm located in the heart of the nearby Covent Garden area! It's amazing.

PART 4
[Feasting]

Food Made With Love

Contrary to popular belief, eating well in London is not difficult at all. Gone are the days when mushy peas (an actual dish) and haggis (don't ask) were the norm. There has evidently been a food explosion, with native and international menus being served with culinary pride all over the city. Feasting here without spending a king's ransom can be a challenging thing, however. But it's our goal to send you to restaurants where you'll be left with the impression that you dined well and also got your money's worth.

Sunday nights tend to be when most Londoners eat at home with their family, and because of this you'll notice that some restaurants are closed or have shorter hours on that night. But in general, Londoners are now so keen on dining out that most of our top picks will now need an advance reservation. Whether you end up in one of ours or not, follow this general guideline: check the menu before you go inside and avoid those places which seem to cater especially to tourists.

All the places listed here have delicious food made with love and are definitely worth finding.

Dining Clue:

Unlike restaurants in European countries, the table isn't yours for the entire evening and you'll be politely asked to finish up after two hours' time. Many reservation confirmations will remind you of this so don't be put off by it, it's perfectly normal. And if you're a party of six or more, London restaurants will usually extend it to 2 1/2 hours. You've got better things to do than just sit in a restaurant all night anyway.

During the Holiday Season:

Many restaurants, like most of London's museums and sights, are closed in order to observe Christmas. For dining on that day, your best bet is to seek out a restaurant inside a major hotel.

Andie says,

"The shrimp served to you in restaurants here will be a goodly size but will almost always be presented on the plate complete with their eyes, tail, shell, and spindly leg things. If you're not used to this it can be off-putting. You can request that the chef peel it all off for you –some kitchens will comply and some won't."

Tender pork loin with yams and broccoli at The Jugged Hare

The Jugged Hare

Centrally located in the streets north of the Museum of London, this unique gastropub serves true British dishes reminiscent of centuries past. The cuisine is so fine however that we imagine this is how The King must have eaten. The menu changes with the seasons depending upon what game is most plentiful. Enjoy their namesake specialty (think *Coq au Vin* made with rabbit) or a tasty Squirrel and Bacon Croquette. Their Mock Turtle Soup is exquisite, as is seemingly *everything* they make.

If your taste buds tend more toward the ordinary, don't fret; this place excels with everything they cook, even if it's merely a steak, pork loin, roast chicken, or cheeseburger. On Sundays they go full out with something the British call a *Sunday Roast* feast. This is a restaurant you should not miss.

Reservations necessary

www.thejuggedhare.com

£££-££££
Ambience: Modern Pub
Noise level: Medium to loud
Lighting: Dim

Credit Cards: Yes
Accessible: No
WiFi: No

Located at 49 Chiswell Street
In The City, London

Intl. calling: (011) 44-20 7614 0134
Local calling: 7614 0134
Local mobile calling: 020 7614 0134

The Jugged Hare is open daily for lunch and dinner
Check their live online booking calendar for available dates and times

Get a Clue:

Save room for one of their special seasonal desserts.

Dean says,

"When you see the mounted deer head through the window, you've arrived."

Andie says,

"Try something daring… you'll be surprised at how delicious this food is."

Clothing Clue:

The dress code for this restaurant is smart casual.

Mother Mash

The ultimate comfort food can be found just up the street from Piccadilly Circus. Oh my but this food is good! Featuring the famous English meal of Bangers & Mash (sausages and mashed potatoes), Mother Mash has made an art of it. And there are plenty of other savory selections as well. The potatoes are whipped and made when you order them, creating the creamiest consistency. Choose your sausage, potato style, and gravy type and dine well for about £10!

Reservations accepted online or by phone

www.mothermash.co.uk

£-££
Ambience: Casual cabin
Noise level: Medium
Lighting: Standard

Credit Cards: Yes
Accessible: Yes
WiFi: No

Located at 26 Ganton Street
-in Soho/ Piccadilly, London

Intl. calling: (011) 44-20 7494 9644
Local landline calling: 7494 9644
Local mobile calling: 020 7494 9644

Open daily for lunch and dinner
Call ahead for hours on major holidays

Dean says,

"Mother Mash is my favorite lunch in all of London. It's incredibly delicious and they have homemade desserts as well."

Andie says,

"There are five types of gravy to choose from but I insist you order the Farmer's Gravy, made with red wine, onions, and bacon."

Clothing Clue:

The dress code for this restaurant is casual.

Gloria

Say hello to our new favorite *Italian* restaurant in London. Ristorante Gloria in Shoreditch is cool. Super cool. It's also beautiful, tasty, friendly, and well-priced for the experience. What more could you want? The menu offers some fun and unexpected items but remains extraordinarily approachable. There is definitely something for everyone. The best part about it is that everyone there seems to be having a great time; even the chefs! If you have room for dessert, try the gravity-resisting lemon pie. Buon appetito!

Reservations taken for both lunch and dinner (but walk-ins are welcome)

www.bigmammagroup.com/en/trattorias/gloria

£££-££££
Ambience: Modern chic
Noise level: Medium to loud
Lighting: Dim
Full bar

Credit Cards: Yes
Accessible: Yes
WiFi: Yes

Located at 54 Great Eastern Street
-in Shoreditch, London

No telephone

Open daily for lunch, dinner, and Sunday brunch
Closed on some major holidays

Dean says,

"Come to see and be seen with London's foodie crowd. Their online reservations open up three weeks before the available date, so be aware."

Andie says,

"I love their creative approach to Italian cuisine."

Clothing Clue:

The dress code for this restaurant is smart casual to a bit dressy.

Dishoom

When one considers England's long and historic connection with India it seems natural to have Indian food while in London. And Dishoom is like the Bombay cafés of old, with a bit more polish of course. There's a reason this bustling restaurant has velvet stanchions at the entrance. The demand for its rich, satisfying Indian fare outweighs the number of tables and so the crowd patiently waits. Don't get us wrong; Dishoom's Covent Garden location isn't small... it's just that the food is *that* good. Spicy and succulent dishes abound so your only dilemma here will be what to order. They feature a tasty breakfast as well, with bottomless Chai tea!

Reservations required for indoor dining
Outdoor dining remains for walk-ins only

www.dishoom.com/covent-garden

££-£££
Ambience: Upscale Bombay Café
Noise level: Medium to loud
Lighting: Dim
Full bar

Credit Cards: Yes
Accessible: Yes
WiFi: Yes

Located at 12 Upper St. Martin's Lane
-in Covent Garden, London

Intl. calling: (011) 44-20 7420 9320
Local landline calling: 7420 9320
Local mobile calling: 020 7420 9320

Dishoom is open daily for breakfast, lunch, and dinner
Closed on Christmas Day, December 26, New Year's Day, and January 2nd

Andie says,

"Another top Indian restaurant happens to be London's oldest and most elegant. Visit Veeraswamy, perfect for a special occasion. It's located at 99 Regent Street."

Dean says,

"Don't forget to order some of Dishoom's handmade *naan* & *roti,* and for an unusual dessert try Memsahib's Mess."

Clothing Clue:

The dress code for this restaurant is smart casual.

Thai Square

Exquisite Thai cuisine is what you get every time at Thai Square. We absolutely love it and think it's worth every penny of the exchange rate. That's saying a lot! Their location on Cockspur Street near Trafalgar Square makes for the perfect pre-theatre meal but their other locations are worth mentioning as well. While all three have a different interior design, each is special in its own way. If you're craving Thai food, treat yourself to a fine meal here.

Reservations usually necessary for dinner

https://thaisq.com

££-£££
Ambience: Upscale Urban
Noise level: Medium to loud
Lighting: Soft
Full bar

Credit Cards: Yes
Accessible: Yes
WiFi: Yes

Located at 21 Cockspur Street
Near Trafalgar Square
St. James's, London

Intl. calling: (011) 44-20 7839 4000
Local landline calling: 7839 4000
Local mobile calling: 020 7839 4000

Open daily for lunch or dinner

Andie says,

"If you like spicy food then you should order their green curry with sticky rice. It's to die for."

Dean says,

"They have a large appetizer platter in case you can't decide on what to start with. We really do love this restaurant; the décor is just beautiful."

Clothing Clue:

The dress code for this restaurant is smart casual.

Chotto Matte

Japanese cuisine with Peruvian influences makes Chotto Matte truly exceptional. The artistic, sexy food being made by their talented chef will make any meal seem like a special occasion. The many sushi offerings and vegetable creations are a feast for the eye and the stomach. The dining room is truly hip and attracts a sophisticated crowd on the weekends.

Reservations usually necessary

www.chotto-matte.com

££-££££
Ambience: Upscale Urban
Noise level: Medium to loud
Lighting: Romantic
Full bar

Credit Cards: Yes
Accessible: Yes
WiFi: Yes

Located at 11 Frith Street
-in Soho, London

Intl. calling: (011) 44-20 7042 7171
Local landline calling: 7042 7171
Local mobile calling: 020 7042 7171
or alternatively, 079 028 220 73

Open daily for lunch or dinner
Closed on some major holidays

Andie says,

"Try several of their gorgeous starters, like Vegetable Tartar or Kumquat Tostaditas."

Dean says,

"The Nikkei barbeque is exotic and satisfying. And their special sharing menus offer diners a great overview of this beautiful cuisine."

Clothing Clue:

The dress code for this restaurant is smart casual to a bit dressy.

Gaucho

For us, an evening at Gaucho is a London requirement. Argentinean at its core, this restaurant is much more refined than a Churrascaria and presents aged beef in many cuts, including filets and rib eyes in a variety of sizes. The handmade sauces and chimichurris are like icing on the cake at this gorgeous space which will have you coming back again and again. For you traditional types we heartily recommend the filet accompanied by their wonderful Béarnaise sauce. The wine list is exemplary and the knowledgeable staff will make certain you have the best vintage for your palette.

Reservations recommended

https://gauchorestaurants.com/restaurants/piccadilly

££££-£££££
Ambience: Elegant Cowboy
Noise level: Medium
Lighting: Dim
Full bar

Credit Cards: Yes
Accessible: Yes
WiFi: Yes

Located at 25 Swallow Street
-near Regent Street
Piccadilly, London

Intl. calling: (011) 44-20 7734 4040
Local landline calling: 7734 4040
Local mobile calling: 020 7734 4040

Gaucho is open daily for lunch and dinner
Closed on some major holidays

Andie says,

"If you like a really thick filet, tell your server that you don't want the chef to butterfly it."

Dean says,

"This is my kind of steak house...friendly, not snooty."

Clothing Clue:

The dress code for this restaurant is smart casual to a bit dressy.

Galvin HOP

Inside a stunning gastropub, Michelin star chef Chris Galvin has made the cuisine here into something really special. Alsatian dishes and fresh Czech Pilsner beer come together for a taste sensation, and they do a killer Tart Tatin too. Quirky starters also prevail in this very creative restaurant located near the old Victorian Spitalfields Market, just north of The City.

Reservations suggested for dinner

https://galvinrestaurants.com/restaurants/galvin-hop-spitalfields

££-£££
Ambience: Upscale Gastropub
Noise level: Medium
Lighting: Standard

Credit Cards: Yes
Accessible: Yes
WiFi: Yes
Full bar

Located at 35 Spital Square
-in Spitalfields, London
Entrance on Bishop's Square

Intl. calling: (011) 44-20 7299 0404
Local landline calling: 7299 0404
Local mobile calling: 020 7299 0404

Open Monday through Saturday for lunch and dinner
Open Sundays for lunch only

Sarastro

You'll have to reserve weeks ahead if you want to dine at Sarastro after a Saturday night performance at the nearby Royal Opera House. This place can easily turn into a party given by someone's gypsy aunt inside her eclectic caravan…or something like that. It's hard to describe Sarastro, which is named for one of Mozart's zany characters in *The Magic Flute*. Serving up Turkish and Mediterranean favorites to happy people is what they do best. Lamb and eggplant (called aubergine in England) weigh heavily on the menu. Really hungry? Try one of their huge pasta dishes, like the seafood linguine.

Reservations recommended

www.sarastro-restaurant.com

£££
Ambience: Flamboyant Gypsy Theatre
Noise level: Medium to loud
Lighting: Romantic
Full bar

Credit Cards: Yes
Accessible: Yes but call ahead
WiFi: Yes

Located at 126 Drury Lane
-in Covent Garden, London

Intl. calling: (011) 44-20 7836 0101
Local landline calling: 7836 0101
Local mobile calling: 020 7836 0101

Open daily for lunch and dinner
Closed on some major holidays

Andie says,

"Oh my! The murals on the walls of the ladies loo are worth a look."

Dean says,

"I was gong to say the same thing about the men's room!"

Get a Clue:

Sarastro was voted one of London's weirdest restaurants but not because of the food. Go there and find out why because we're not going to be the ones to let the cat out of the bag.

Clothing Clue:

The dress code for this restaurant is smart casual.

Sketch –for Afternoon Tea

What can we say about Sketch… that it's fabulous? Yes, but that kind of goes without saying. Their townhouse-turned-outrageous, members-only club houses a bar, a cocktail lounge, and three restaurants, one of which is indeed strictly private. We non-member mortals are welcome to partake in the savory and sweet goodies inside The Gallery, which is undoubtedly one of the most beautiful pink tea rooms in the world. And their tea service is worthy of it.

Reservations necessary, by phone or online

https://sketch.london

£££
Ambience: Chic fifties
Noise level: Medium
Lighting: Medium

Credit Cards: Yes
Accessible: Yes
WiFi: Yes
Full bar

Located at 9 Conduit Street
-in Mayfair, London

Intl. Calling: (011) 44-20 7659 4500
Local mobile calling: 0207 659 4500

Afternoon Tea served in *The Gallery* daily, with live music *Friday through Sunday*

Rapsa @ 100 Hoxton

This casual restaurant is crazy at brunch time… like crazy *good!* Their Filipino fusion cuisine is really interesting and packed with flavor. Go there on a Sunday morning for colorful egg dishes or a huge sharing platter which lets you sample many of the tasty goodies coming out of the kitchen here. It's about beautiful food and creative cocktails.

Reservations recommended

https://rapsa.co.uk

££-£££
Ambience: Filipino brasserie
Noise level: Medium to Loud
Lighting: Dim

Credit Cards: Yes
Accessible: Yes
WiFi: No
Full bar

Located at 100 Hoxton Street
-in Shoreditch, London
North of *The City*

Intl. calling: (011) 44-20 7729 1444
Local landline calling: 7729 1444
Local mobile calling: 020 7729 1444

Open Tuesday through Sunday from early to late
Closed Mondays and some major holidays

Afternoon Tea at The Royal Crescent
(in Bath, England)

If you want a quintessential Afternoon Tea experience done in the elegant, Georgian, country-manners way, then take the ninety minute train to Bath (which conveniently delivers you right to the center of town.) There, The Royal Crescent Hotel will make you feel as if you have gone back to a gentler time.

In their exquisite tea house, with a view of an English garden, you'll be served savories and sweets worthy of royalty. Each guest may choose from a variety of tea menus which include fruit infusions as well as tea or coffee. Want more of something on the plate? Just ask!

This is our favorite thing to do in Bath, and is about half the price of having Afternoon Tea in London at one of the fancy hotels. Still, there are many worthy in London if you feel like staying put. We like the one at the Hotel Savoy.

Pre-booking by telephone is essential to insure a table

www.royalcrescent.co.uk/afternoon-tea

£££
Ambience: White tablecloth elegance
Noise level: Soft
Lighting: Romantic
Full bar

Credit Cards: Yes
Accessible: Yes
WiFi: Yes

Located at 16 Royal Crescent
-in Bath, Somerset, England

Intl. Calling: (011) 44 1225 823 333
Local landline calling: 1225 823 333

Afternoon Tea presented daily indoors or in the garden

Train Clue:

From London's Paddington Station, direct train service to Bath Spa departs many times a day. Book ahead if possible at:

www.thetrainline.com/train-times/london-paddington-to-bath-spa

Andie says,

"Bath Buns are my new reason for living and these apple-stuffed delights are fantastic here at the Royal Crescent. I must also mention their exquisite warm mushroom croquettes!"

Dean says,

"I've discovered that I like finger sandwiches."

Clothing Clue:

The dress code for this restaurant is smart casual to a bit dressy.

Hotel Clue:

If you're staying overnight in Bath, consider The Royal Crescent Hotel & Spa for your accommodation. It's located on the loveliest street in England and is truly like being in another world.

PART 5

[The Pub Report]

Featuring our Historic Pub Crawl

You can hardly plan a visit to London without giving some thought as to which pubs (short for *public house*) you should patronize. The number of pubs in London is actually astounding; there seems to be one every few blocks. You'll undoubtedly end up inside one, probably one that happens to be where you are at the time or whichever is nearest your accommodation. If you're staying in Westminster then be sure to stop at The Red Lion which gets our vote for prettiest pub.

For a more intense experience, we present The Pub Report (unique to this edition of our *Clued In Travel* series.) This is a recommended pub crawl of four historic and fun pubs. We think it's great for several reasons... first, all of these pubs are very old and very famous; second, they're all conveniently within a few blocks of each other near the north side of Blackfriar's Bridge; and third, they all serve food. So if you get hungry –or too tipsy– along the way, don't fret. By the way, it doesn't really matter which one you start at but we think it works best in the order listed.

Clued In London's HISTORIC PUB CRAWL

Ye Olde Cheshire Cheese *(Est. 1538)*

Ye Olde London *(Est. 1749)*

The Cockpit *(Est. 1798)*

The Black Friar *(Est. 1875)*

118

Ye Olde Cheshire Cheese

By all accounts this is the oldest pub in London. Though established in 1538, it had to be completely rebuilt after the great fire of 1666. Today it still stands and harkens back to the days when Charles Dickens used to drink his ale there. There's evidence that the top level was used as a brothel in the 1700's. Dark and gloomy to some, we love its interior... seemingly untouched by time. Have the first beer here and pray you don't run into Sweeny Todd.

~145 Fleet Street / Local mobile call: 020 7353-6170

Ye Olde London

Yes, Benjamin Franklin really did drink at this pub during his visit to London. Today it looks old but feels new, its cheerful interior persuading guests to belly up to the bar for real London ale. Yes Americans, they do serve nachos.

~42 Ludgate Hill / Local mobile call: 020 7248-1852

The Cockpit

This tiny corner pub is as historic as it gets, and folks from the neighborhood happily crowd up to the bar for a beer. In the early 1600's, Shakespeare owned and lived in a building on this very spot. When a pub was built here instead, a gallery was installed so that spectators could view and gamble on the cock fights which were regularly held. The brutal fights were finally banned in 1849.

~7 St. Andrews Hill / Local mobile call: 020 7248-7315

The Black Friar Public House

If you're not too drunk by the time you get to The Black Friar then take a moment to notice how absolutely gorgeous it is. Handpicked ales from the best breweries in Britain can be savored here, under stunning décor which looks properly old but in a royal kind of way. The friar sculptures are by Henry Poole. Superb!

~174 Queen Victoria Street / Local cell call: 020 7236-5474

Cultural Clue:

These historic pubs are open everyday but close by 11pm, earlier on Sundays. Do your crawl in the late afternoon if you can.

Mealtime Clue:

Some pubs in The City area don't serve food on the weekend. People just want to drink and that's all.

Pro Tip:

There are basically two kinds of beer: *lagers* and *ales*. Lagers are brewed with bottom-fermenting yeast and have a lighter, smoother quality...ales are brewed with top-fermenting yeast and are more robust and intense. Ale has been around for more than 2,000 years while lager first appeared sometime in the eighteenth-century. A Pilsner, by the way, is a lager with those spicy hops added to it.

Get a Clue: Fish & Chips

While moderately priced from £11 to £16, the famed English meal of Fish and Chips seems a no-brainer as far as eating in London is concerned, especially in a pub. You might be disappointed however, as the recipe has changed since days of old. The fish served to you these days has most likely been frozen and while still dipped in batter, it's now fried in standard vegetable oil. This makes for a tasteless dish which barely resembles what made it famous in the first place.

The old recipe (from Yorkshire) was a white fish, freshly caught, battered and fried in meat suet which added a rich, complex flavor. The chips (Brit-speak for thick potato wedges) were fried in the same fatty goodness. This method is largely gone in London thanks to health-conscious eaters, vegetarians, and frugal chefs. If you simply must order this dish then be ready with the malt vinegar, salt, tarter sauce and perhaps ketchup in order to give it some kind of flavor. Or order an English meat pie instead. By the way, it's British law that the establishment must inform the public as to what specific kind of fish is being served. We've found that it's usually cod.

PART 6

[Treats]

From Bakeries to Booze

Harrods' Food Halls have everything you could want

Harrods' Food Halls

If there's one lasting memory you might have of London, the unbelievable food halls at Harrods might be it. Picture not one, but four enormous, shining, elegant rooms filled with the most beautiful foods and delectable food products you have ever seen in one place. From stuffed dates in ten varieties to gnarly heirloom tomatoes, you can find anything and everything there. Teas, jams, sushi, chocolate, breads, and prepared recipes… it's simply astounding. Luckily, there are many inexpensive items to bring home.

Located on the street level, just past the perfume room

www.harrods.com

Free to visit

£-£££
Credit Cards: Yes
Accessible: Yes
WiFi: Yes
Take out: Yes

Located at 87-135 Brompton Road
-in Knightsbridge, London

Intl. calling: (011) 44-20 8479 5100
Local landline calling: 8479 5100
Local mobile calling: 020 8479 5100

Open daily
Closed on Christmas Day

Pro Tip:

Forget those tacky souvenir shops. This is the place to find gifts for loved ones! The food halls offer boxed chocolates, jars of gourmet fruit preserves, international teas, and a thousand other things you've never thought of before. Some are priced as little as £3 even though the packaging is expensive-looking.

Mealtime Clue:

The Food Halls offer several restaurants which are dispersed throughout and vary in price and cuisine.

Historical Highlight:

Harrods was founded in 1834.

Bakeries

Paul

A real French bakery and patisserie, Paul never fails to make our recommendation list when located in a city we're reviewing. It's owned by the same company as the Ladurée Macarons which should tell you something. And yes, that previous photo shows one of our actual breakfasts just moments before we devoured it all.

Paul does offer more than just baked goods though, and everything is top notch. They have freshly baked breads, sandwiches, salads, and beverages, all of which can be enjoyed right inside at a comfortable table or packed to go. (A picnic in Hyde Park perhaps?) We love a brie and baguette sandwich first thing in the morning as a European style breakfast before starting our sight-seeing itinerary.

£-££
Credit Cards: Yes
Accessible: Usually
WiFi: Usually

Paul has many London locations. Here's one of them:

PAUL
Located in the Piccadilly Arcade
-in St. James's, London
Intl calling: (011) 44-20 3978 5525
Local landline calling: 3978 5525
Local mobile calling: 020 3978 5525

Open daily

Dean says,

"Their various locations have different opening hours based on the area."

Andie says,

"Paul boulangerie & patisserie has been baking since 1889. For me it offers the very best quality for shops of this kind."

Bageriet Bakery

Is there anything as wonderful as a really great Swedish bakery? We don't think so. And luckily there's one right in the centrally-located Covent Garden neighborhood.

Bageriet is tucked into an almost secret alleyway called Rose Street, so you'll have to look for the entrance pathway from Long Acre Street. It sounds more difficult than it is. The payoff is huge: flaky, buttery breakfast treats and real marzipan Princess Cakes await you. It's simply fantastic!

www.bageriet.co.uk

£-££
Credit Cards: Yes
Accessible: No, but the staff will take your order
WiFi: No

Located at 24 Rose Street
In Covent Garden, London

Intl. calling: (011) 44-20 7240 0000
Local landline calling: 7240 0000
Local mobile calling: 020 7240 0000

Closed Sunday and Mondays
Closed on some major holidays

Andie says,

"They have only one location so you might find there's a bit of a wait. Worth every minute though."

Dean says,

"They currently offer outdoor seating but can pack up your purchase to take with you if you prefer."

Cutter & Squidge

When it's cake we're craving, we head over to some of the best in town. At Cutter & Squidge bakery on historic Brewer Street, the cakes are big and the cakes are delicious! They even offer many gorgeous vegan varieties. They bake other wonderful pastries here too of course, and offer up some lovely cups of tea -but it's the cakes we truly long for. You'll understand when you see them.

https://cutterandsquidge.com

£-££
Credit Cards: Yes
Accessible: Yes
WiFi: No

Located at 20 Brewer Street
In the heart of Soho, London

Intl. calling: (011) 44-20 7734 2540
Local landline calling: 7734 2540
Local mobile calling: 020 7734 2540

Open daily from 11am
Closed on some major holidays

Dean says,
"Not into big cake slices? Try their specialty dessert instead. It's called the Biskie -it's a sandwich cookie filled with fruits and buttercream."

131

Ice Cream

Gelupo

Ice cream might not be the first thing to come to mind when one thinks of London but trust us; they have some very fine ice cream indeed. Behind a quaint storefront on narrow Archer Street (just a short stroll from Piccadilly Circus) you'll find the best ice cream in the British capital. Gelupo has been serving it up according to their strict quality recipes since 2010. Their fresh, seasonal, ever-changing flavors keep visitors coming back. Try the Fresh Mint Stracciatella or Ricotta Sour Cherry (if you can get it) and let your tastebuds sing.

www.gelupo.com

£-££
Credit Cards: Yes
Accessible: Yes
WiFi: No

Located at 7 Archer Street
-near Piccadilly Circus, London

Intl. calling: (011) 44-20 7287 5555
Local landline calling: 7287 5555
Local mobile calling: 020 7287 5555

Open daily and nightly
Closed on some major holidays

Dean says,

"This adorable gelato shop is the brainchild of award-winning chef Jacob Kenedy who also owns the Italian restaurant Bocca di Lupo right across the street."

Andie says,

"Want something lighter? The Gelupo shop also offers amazing sorbets."

Cheeses

Paxton & Whitfield

This delightful shop, just steps from Piccadilly Circus, has the stinky cheeses you're looking for. They also have just about any other cheese you could possibly want, as well as gourmet condiments and sandwiches. Their history as a premium cheesemonger spans some 200 years. The wonderful aroma will tell you that you have arrived.

www.paxtonandwhitfield.co.uk/visit-us

£-£££
Credit Cards: Yes
Accessible: Yes
WiFi: No

Located at 93 Jermyn Street
-in the St. James's area, London

Intl. calling: (011) 44-20 7930 0259
Local landline calling: 7930 0259
Local mobile calling: 020 7930 0259

Open Monday through Saturday
Closed on Sundays, and some major holidays

Dean says,
"If you find yourself on Jermyn Street, make sure you stop in to experience this exquisite and historical shop."

Cocktails

Nightjar

In case you skipped Part 1, we need to make sure you know about Nightjar speakeasy. Their unique, award-winning cocktails are the best in the world today. Make a booking well in advance to reserve a table. Their No Standing policy means an uncrowded atmosphere so that you can relax, have fun, and appreciate the wonderful service. Order up tasty tapas or a charcuterie plate to nibble on while you enjoy their extensive cocktail list. Live jazz and old-school piano complete the ambiance in this fun, sophisticated, relaxed and unusual place. It makes for a truly great night out.

Note: Its address here in Shoreditch isn't easy to find, so we should mention that it's just north of a large traffic circle dominating the area... walk along until your see the red awning of Chicken Cottage and then spy the dark wooden doors with a plaque of a little Nightjar bird. It's between Café Arena and KFC. Consider yourself informed, again.

Reservations are now required, in advance

https://barnightjar.com

££-£££
Ambience: Hip glamour grunge
Noise level: Medium to loud
Lighting: Dim

Credit Cards: Yes
Accessible: No
WiFi: No

Located at 129 City Road
-in Shoreditch, London

Intl. calling: (011) 44-20 7253 4101
Local landline calling: 7253 4101
Local mobile calling: 020 7253 4101

Open nightly
Closed on some major holidays

Andie says,

"Their cocktail menu is ever changing but you'll find one that's right for you."

Dean says,

"This is one of those places where planning ahead matters, and where you'll be rewarded for having some kind of dining and entertainment itinerary."

Pro Tip:

There are now two Nightjar speakeasies in London. Their newest location is located right in the quaint and very-central tourist area of Carnaby which couldn't be more convenient. It is smaller than the original in Shoreditch but has the same great mixology. (Being the purists that we are, we prefer the one in Shoreditch.) If you can't get a reservation at one then try the other.

PART 7

[Accommodations]

Hotels to Set the Mood

Where you stay will set the mood for your entire visit, even if you don't end up spending much time there. Just leaving from, or returning to, a beautiful hotel gives the traveler an indescribable feeling. We recommend that first-time visitors to London stay at a hotel in the city center in a neighborhood that really appeals to them.

Walk in the footsteps of Oscar Wilde at The Langham, rub elbows with celebrities at the glamorous Hotel Bvlgari, or if you're on more of a budget you might consider a smaller boutique hotel like the Fielding. Go online and find them. Some will raise their prices in the summer or during major festival days so consider the calendar when choosing your time to visit. (Details in the chapter titled *Some Final Clues*)

Hotels vs. online apartment rentals:

While the popularity of renting apartments through particular websites continues to grow, remember that hotels offer *services* and that's part of what you're paying for. A hotel stay might suit your party better than an apartment stay. The trick is to think about what kind of vacation experience you're seeking in London… don't need help with the language? Don't care about a complimentary breakfast buffet? Don't need concierge services, or possible medical attention? Don't need access to a room safe? Don't need free bicycles, babysitting services, or someone to call a taxi? Not planning on a massage or workout? Then you may not need a hotel.

We know that an independent stay in a private home has its charms – just be smart about what you're giving up; if it suits you, terrific; Airbnb is quite reliable here. But it'll never compare to the experience of a truly great hotel.

Pro Tip:

The star ratings of hotels are *not* generated by a consensus of people's opinions. They are actually a strict industry rating, based on a particular hotel's guest services and capabilities. For instance, two very similar hotels can be rated 3 stars or 4 stars depending if one has a restaurant. This system is meant to help you choose a hotel with the level of service and amenities you desire.

Andie says,

"All of the hotels recommended below have complimentary bath products, blow dryers, and ironing boards so don't stress when you don't see them on the amenity lists."

A Little Stair Scare:

Most of London's hotels are accessible for those with limited mobility.

*The exquisite Royal Horseguards Hotel
and Whitehall Gardens*

The Royal Horseguards Hotel (5 star)

This chateau-like palace may not be very English in style but it's one of the most beautiful buildings in London. Perfectly located along the north edge of the River Thames, it's loaded with history. It was the secret service headquarters for decades. Renovated as a prestigious Guoman hotel in 2009, it's well-priced for its comfort and style. It offers first-rate concierge services and amenities, and the Royal Horseguards staff will pamper you every way they can.

- ✓ Centrally located to all of Westminster
- ✓ Near Trafalgar Square
- ✓ Close to many shops and restaurants
- ✓ Award-winning restaurant
- ✓ Terrace dining and cocktail lounges
- ✓ Sweeping views
- ✓ Newly renovated rooms
- ✓ Private modern baths
- ✓ Air conditioning
- ✓ Satellite TV service
- ✓ Bathrobes
- ✓ Egyptian cotton bed linens
- ✓ Mini bar
- ✓ Large room safe with internal laptop charging
- ✓ Concierge services
- ✓ Breakfast offered for an additional fee
- ✓ Free WiFi
- ✓ Valet parking available
- ✓ Two-hundred eighty-two rooms

www.guoman.com

££-££££

Located at 2 Whitehall Court
-in Westminster, London
Entrance on the north side of the building

Intl. calling: (011) 44-20 7523 5062
Local landline calling: 7523 5062
Local mobile calling: 020 7523 5062

Direct email is available through their website

Bvlgari Hotel (5 star)

The Bvlgari London is relatively new and offers an austere elegance that's missing at most of the more expensive British hotels. Not that there's anything wrong with the aesthetic of London's "usual suspects," but if you want a truly modern, 21st-century accommodation with the most advanced spa services in the UK, then this is your place. All this, and walkable to Harrods and Harvey Nichols!

- ✓ Located in the ritzy Hyde Park area
- ✓ Walking distance to Mayfair's best boutiques
- ✓ The Bvlgari Spa
- ✓ Restaurant and two cocktail lounges
- ✓ New, stylish rooms
- ✓ Private modern baths
- ✓ Air conditioning
- ✓ 42" LCD TVs
- ✓ Bathrobes
- ✓ Egyptian cotton bed linens
- ✓ Nespresso coffeemaker
- ✓ In-room safe
- ✓ Bvlgari toiletries & amenities
- ✓ Hair salon
- ✓ Fitness center and pool
- ✓ Concierge services
- ✓ Breakfast buffet offered
- ✓ Free WiFi
- ✓ Valet parking
- ✓ Eighty-five guestrooms

www.bulgarihotels.com/london

££££-£££££

Located at 171 Knightsbridge
-in Mayfair, London

Intl. calling: (011) 44-20 7151 1010
Local landline calling: 7151 1010
Local mobile calling: 020 7151 1010

Email: london@bulgarihotels.co.uk

Radisson Blu Edwardian - Mercer Street (4 star)

We say *Mercer Street* because there are two different Radisson Blu hotels in London. This one will place you at the edge of our preferred neighborhood of Covent Garden. Here you'll be very central and walking distance to Leicester Square, the West End shows, the Royal Opera House, Piccadilly Square, Chinatown, Soho shopping, and even the British Museum. We adore it and believe it's the best choice in London for the mid-range price category. You'll feel spoiled here.

- ✓ Centrally located in the Seven Dials/Covent Garden area
- ✓ Walking distance to many top sights
- ✓ Restaurant and cocktail lounge
- ✓ Lovely modern rooms
- ✓ Private modern baths
- ✓ Air conditioning
- ✓ Flat-screen HD-TV
- ✓ Imported bed linens
- ✓ REN toiletries
- ✓ Mini bar and Nespresso coffee machine
- ✓ In-room safe
- ✓ Concierge services
- ✓ Excellent breakfast buffet usually included
- ✓ Free WiFi
- ✓ Complimentary bottled water
- ✓ Room service
- ✓ 24-hour fitness center
- ✓ Accessible rooms available
- ✓ One-hundred thirty-seven rooms and suites

**www.radissonhotels.com/en-us/hotels/
radisson-blu-edwardian-london-mercer-street**

£££-££££

Located at 20 Mercer Street
-in Seven Dials/ Covent Garden, London

Intl. calling: (011) 44-20 7836 4300
Local landline calling: 7836 4300
Local mobile calling: 020 7836 4300

Email: resmerc@radisson.com

The Langham London (5 star)
A Leading Hotels of the World

There's no argument about whether the Langham is London's Victorian Grand Dame. Built in 1865 as a splendid five-hundred room hotel, it has played host to such literary luminaries as Arthur Conan Doyle and Oscar Wilde.

This elegant and historic place is also said to be one of the most haunted in London, but you may or may not encounter ghosts as you relax in your gorgeous renovated room or suite. Full of history, the Langham boasts the original Palm Court Restaurant where an elegant afternoon tea was first created.

As far as location, The Langham is barely within our centralized London ideal. But it offers so much in the way of services that you should look past this. Visit the website below for special offers.

- ✓ Located near Oxford street shopping
- ✓ Walking distance to Regent's Park
- ✓ Spa and swimming pool
- ✓ Two restaurants and a cocktail lounge
- ✓ Traditional, upscale rooms
- ✓ Private modern baths
- ✓ Air conditioning
- ✓ Flat screen TVs
- ✓ Bathrobes
- ✓ Premium bed linens
- ✓ In-room tea and coffeemaker
- ✓ Complimentary bottled water
- ✓ In-room Safe
- ✓ Complimentary toiletries

- ✓ 24-hour room service
- ✓ Concierge services
- ✓ Breakfast offered for a fee
- ✓ Free WiFi
- ✓ Valet parking available
- ✓ Three-hundred eighty rooms and suites

www.langhamhotels.com/en/the-langham/london

£££-£££££

Located at 1C Portland Place, at Regent Street
-in Marylebone, London
(You can't miss it)

Intl. calling: (011) 44-20 7636 1000
Local landline calling: 7636 1000
Local mobile calling: 020 7636 1000

Email: tllon.info@langhamhotels.com

Charlotte Street Hotel (4 star)

Just streets away from the British Museum, this lovely hotel is situated north of the fabulous section of town where Crumbs & Doilies bakery and Mother Mash can be found. The Charlotte Street Hotel is a highly-rated contemporary hotel that offers top notch guest services and much, much more. They have a modern screening room and proudly host the Charlotte Hotel Film Club. Visit their website for special room offers and film screening packages. Very cool.

- ✓ Located close to the West End
- ✓ Walking distance to the British Museum
- ✓ Restaurant and a bar
- ✓ English contemporary-styled rooms
- ✓ Private modern baths
- ✓ Air conditioning
- ✓ Flat screen LCD TV
- ✓ DVD player
- ✓ Gym
- ✓ Bathrobes
- ✓ Luxurious *Frette* bed linens
- ✓ Mini bar
- ✓ In-room Safe
- ✓ Complimentary toiletries
- ✓ Complimentary bottled water
- ✓ 24-hour room service
- ✓ Concierge services
- ✓ Breakfast available
- ✓ Free WiFi
- ✓ Valet parking available
- ✓ Fifty-two guest rooms

www.firmdalehotels.com/hotels/london/charlotte-street-hotel

£££-££££

Located at 15 Charlotte Street
-in Fitzrovia/ Bloomsbury, London

Intl. calling: (011) 44-20 7806 2000
Local landline calling: 7806 2000
Local mobile calling: 020 7806 2000

Email: reservations@charlottestreethotel.com

The Fielding Hotel (3.5 stars)

The Fielding is our top choice for an inexpensive hotel with the best location possible. It has a charming and quaint appeal, and is located in Covent Garden which is one of the pricier neighborhoods. The Fielding is only a short stroll to many of the West End theatres, the famous Somerset House, and many of our recommended restaurants and sights. Truly in the heart of London for a great price. Included in your room rate is complimentary access to the Covent Garden Spa and Gym Complex complete with lap pool.

- ✓ Located 200' from the Royal Opera House
- ✓ Central to the rest of London
- ✓ Free access to a fitness center
- ✓ Bright, cozy rooms
- ✓ Private bathrooms with tub or shower
- ✓ Air conditioning
- ✓ In-room TVs
- ✓ In-room tea and coffee facilities
- ✓ Hairdryers in all rooms
- ✓ Tube stop 500' away
- ✓ Situated on a pedestrian-only street
- ✓ Free WiFi
- ✓ Twenty-five rooms

www.thefieldinghotel.co.uk

££-£££

Located at 4 Broad Court, between Drury and Bow Streets
-in Covent Garden, London

Intl. calling: (011) 44-20 7836 8305
Local landline calling: 7836 8305
Local mobile calling: 020 7836 8305

Email: reservations@thefieldinghotel.co.uk

PART 8

[All Transport]

Airport Transfers
Buses
Taxis
& the Tube

Whether you're arriving by air or by train, we have a solution for you so that you can get to your accommodation without a hassle.

London Airports

London's two main airports are (LHR) Heathrow International, and (LGW) Gatwick -which is used mainly for flights within the UK and Europe. Getting from either airport to central London is easy, especially by express train. Below are some basic tips, but a wealth of information can be found on their easy-to-use airport websites:

www.heathrow.com

www.gatwickairport.com

Heathrow Express trains speed visitors from the airport to London in style

Getting from Heathrow Airport to London

Take the famous (HEX) Heathrow Express train. This is the fastest way to get to central London. In fifteen minutes you'll arrive at London's Paddington Station. Amazing.

Trains depart every fifteen minutes from Terminals 2, 3 and 5 and are accommodating to those with limited mobility. Book online more than two weeks ahead to get a *substantial* savings at **www.heathrowexpress.com** Children under fifteen (and your luggage) ride free on this train.

Around £25 one way (if purchased last minute)
Around £37 *round trip* (if purchased last minute)

If you book at least 90 days in advance, you can get tickets from around £5.50 one way, but they are limited so do hurry.

Take the new Elizabeth Line train to LHR from Paddington Station (or elsewhere.) Sleek trains arrive right inside the airport terminal. This train line will definitely save you money compared to the Heathrow Express, but it takes thirty-five minutes instead of fifteen. It does have the added advantage of many other stations where you can board, so consider the neighborhood in which you are staying.

Buy tickets at Paddington Station, or beforehand at **https://tfl.gov.uk/modes/elizabeth-line**

Around £11 per person

Grab a taxi from the queue waiting out front of the baggage claim area. (A sign denotes the start of the line.) There's no fixed rate from the airport so your cost will be tracked by the meter. There is a LHR fee of around **£2,80** as well. Your final price will depend on the traffic. It usually takes less than an hour. All London taxis are accommodating to those with limited mobility.

From £60 to £100 *–but one price for up to five passengers*

National Express Bus provides express service to London in modern, air-conditioned coaches. They can be found in front of Terminals 2, 3, 4, and 5 and depart every forty minutes. Tickets can be purchased online at **www.nationalexpress.com** or at ticket machines in the Heathrow central bus station. They may also be operating a ticket office right in the international arrivals area. This is an inexpensive and comfortable choice, but you'll have to endure the traffic for 45 to 60 minutes before arriving at one of their many London stops. These buses are accommodating to those with limited mobility.

Around £10 per person

Take the Piccadilly line Underground "Tube" train. This is very cost effective, especially if you were planning to buy an Oyster Card metro pass anyway. This is only for those who have packed light and have *no* limited mobility. Travel time is 50-60 minutes to central London.

£3 to £6 *–or just load a new Oyster card*

Note: cards are available at the Tube's ticket machines in Terminal 2, 3, 4, and 5.

Getting from Gatwick Airport to London

The roads between Gatwick and central London aren't speedways and must go through many towns and suburbs. This can make travel by taxi or bus a long, tedious journey which is dependant upon the traffic conditions. It's much better to travel by train.

The famous (GEX) Gatwick Express train is operational again but we now prefer the alternate airport train, the **ThamesLink** instead! It's located right at the Gatwick airport and will get you to London Blackfriars for a fair price. Get the *ThamesLink On Track app* for effortless ticketing and current scheduling or just buy your ticket at the handy vending machines in the airport train station. Open seating makes it effortless and there is plenty of space for luggage. We love it. Still, if you want to pay more to save a few minutes then book a ticket for the Gatwick Express.

Around £13 per person for the ThamesLink

Visit **www.thameslinkrailway.com**

Grab a taxi from the queue waiting out front of the baggage claim area. (A sign denotes the start of the line.) There's no fixed rate from the airport so your cost will be tracked by the meter. There is an airport fee of around £2,80 as well. Your final price will depend on the traffic. It usually takes sixty to ninety minutes. All London taxis are accommodating to those with limited mobility.

Around £80 to £140 *–but one price for up to five passengers*

National Express Bus provides express service to London in modern, air-conditioned coaches. They can be found in the lower South Terminal forecourt. Tickets can be purchased online at **www.nationalexpress.com** or at ticket machines in the airport. This is an inexpensive and comfortable choice, but you'll have to endure the traffic for more than two hours before arriving at one of their many London stops. These buses are accommodating to those with limited mobility.

Around £10 per person

Getting from London back to Heathrow or Gatwick airports

Take the Heathrow Express train to LHR from Paddington Station. It arrives right at your airport terminal. Buy tickets at Paddington, or beforehand online at its website: **www.heathrowexpress.com**

Substantial discounts offered for early purchasing!
   Around £25 per person before discounts

Take the new Elizabeth Line train to LHR from Paddington Station (or elsewhere.) Sleek trains arrive right inside the airport terminal. This train line will definitely save you money compared to the Heathrow Express, but it takes thirty-five minutes instead of fifteen. It does have the added advantage of many other stations where you can board, so consider the neighborhood in which you are staying.

Buy tickets at Paddington Station, or beforehand at

https://tfl.gov.uk/modes/elizabeth-line

   Around £11 per person

The famous (GEX) Gatwick Express train is operational again but we now prefer the alternate airport train, the ThamesLink instead! It's located right at Gatwick airport and will get you to London Blackfriars for a fair price. Get the *ThamesLink On Track app* for effortless ticketing and current scheduling or just buy your ticket at the handy vending machines in the airport train station. Open seating makes it effortless and there is plenty of space for luggage. We love it. Still, if you want to pay more to save a few minutes then book a ticket for the Gatwick Express.

Around £13 per person for the ThamesLink train
Visit **www.thameslinkrailway.com**

Hail a taxi from anywhere. They'll be happy take you to either airport. Always look for one with its orange roof light lit up. There's no flat fare so the trip cost will be metered as you go. You can also have your hotel call for one, but remember it will arrive with its cost meter already running a fare.

Around £60 to £150 depending on the airport and time of day– *but one price for up to five passengers*

Ride a National Express Bus from the Victoria Coach Station. Departures from morning to night, at least once an hour. Buy a ticket at the station from one of the automated ticket machines, or beforehand online at **www.nationalexpress.com**

Around £10

What's our favorite method of connecting between London and the airports?

We thought you'd never ask! We can't say enough about London's airport trains; they are fast, convenient, and comfortable –even if you have lots of luggage. After a long flight, all we want to do is get to our hotel, even if just to ditch our bags. These trains are not as inexpensive as the buses but we think they're worth every penny. Buy your tickets way in advance online and you'll receive a *substantial* discount, especially for the Heathrow Express.

Not flying in?

If you're coming in by train from Paris or beyond, then you'll arrive on a Eurostar train at **London's St. Pancras International Station**. From there you can grab a taxi or take an Underground tube train to your accommodation.

Taxi Clues

- Official taxis are usually black and have a sign on top of the vehicle displaying the word TAXI. They have a working meter inside showing the cost as you go along. If the vehicle's sign is lit up then it's available for hire. For your own safety never take unlicensed taxis.

- Taxis can be hailed from anywhere, or can be found in taxi queues near popular areas and at all major train stations. Watch for ones with their taxi light on.

- We have found that London cabbies are very honest in choosing the right route.

- The minimum fare is around £3,20. Rides to the airport, or rides on Christmas or New Year's Day, will come with a small supplemental fee. (There are no fixed rates between London and the airports in either direction.)

- A taxi booked by phone (even by your hotel or restaurant) will also have a supplemental fee and the meter running. This is normal so don't panic.

- Some London taxis accept credit cards but ask the driver *before* you ride.

- No tip is expected but it's polite to simply round up the amount on the meter.

Note: The popular Uber Car service is currently allowed to operate in London, for now. Their contract with the city will expire in March so we must wait to see what happens then.

Tube Clues

London's vast underground train system, affectionately called the Tube, is a fast way to get around. Figuring it out can be a bit daunting however. Even their *pay-as-you-go,* don't worry *your-daily-cost-will-be-capped* and you can get any *extra-monies-refunded-when-you-leave-London* "Oyster Cards" can make a visitor crazy.

Some of the larger Tube stations are an underground maze unto themselves while others are so small that the only ways in and out are via a very questionable-looking elevator (say *lift*) or by a concrete spiral ramp. Spiral ramp not a problem, you say? Most are around 200 steps and take forever to climb. If you ride the Tube only a short distance, perhaps one stop or two, you might find that you're exiting out through a vast labyrinth of the *same* station you started from in the first place. Ugh.

Having said all that, there have been recent improvements. Most stations now have escalators and the Oyster Card is actually quite convenient. Once purchased at a vending machine inside a Tube station, you're ready to go. Just tap it at the electronic reader at the turnstile and then tap it again at your destination's turnstile. It will know how much to deduct. And if you find you've run out of money, insert your card into one of those same vending machines to "top it off" with additional funds.

If you're thinking, "It's so much easier to jump into a taxi or Uber," then you're right –but that taxi or car service will undoubtedly get stuck in a ton of traffic. We do a combination of both modes of transportation depending on how far we're going and what time of day it is. Just use your common sense. One thing is certain though: London is too big to walk everywhere!

Pro Tip:

Use Google Maps' *Directions* on your smart device and then click on the "train" icon. This magically brings up the Line name, Line color, name of the stations at the start and end of your journey, along with the *number* of stops and how long it will take! Once you've looked at this, the line posters of train stops inside the Underground Stations will make perfect sense to you. Just try it.

London Tube map: **http://tfl.gov.uk/maps/track/tube**

- With its 270 stations marked with the word UNDERGROUND, London has one of the most extensive subway systems in the world. It's certainly the oldest. Parts of it date back as far as 1863. These underground trains run every few minutes from 5am to 1am and can get quite crowded during the rush hours.

- There's no Tube service on Christmas Day.

- Tap your Oyster Card (or slip a paper ticket into the turnstile slot) to enter, and make sure to keep it handy in case inspectors should board and ask to see it. *Your card or ticket will also be required in order to exit your destination station!*

- Tube doors open and close automatically at every stop.

- You can transfer to other lines within the Tube system inside stations where they merge.

- Be aware that on wide escalators Londoners stand to the right and walk on the left.

- Tube maps are free so just ask a ticket agent for one or go online and make a screen shot.

- Oyster machines don't give change and will keep any overage. Credit cards are accepted for purchase.

- "Topping off" means adding money to your travel card.

- "Mind the gap" means to watch your step getting on or off; some underground stations have quite a gap between the train and the platform.

- Keep your valuables (wallet, smart-phone) secure and tucked out of sight

- The Underground train system is accommodating to those with limited mobility *in certain stations*. Check their official website for specifics.

City Buses

Bus lines in central London are fairly straightforward but do require a pay-as-you-go Travel Card, or the Oyster Card, in order to board. The buses are almost all double-decker and can be a good way to see the city as you head towards a particular destination.

These travel cards can be purchased from the same self-ticketing machines that service the Tube Underground trains, or at a service window. Remember to queue up properly at bus stops because there's no random-order boarding in Britain.

PART 9

[Some Final Clues]

Free Sights
Festivals
LGBTQ
Tipping
& Safety

The King's sentry outside Buckingham Palace

The Top Free Museums:

British Museum*
Courtauld Gallery
Imperial War Museum
Museum of London
National Army Museum
National Gallery*
National Maritime Museum
National Portrait Gallery (*closed for reno until June 2023*)
Natural History Museum
Saatchi Gallery of Contemporary Art
Science Museum
Serpentine Modern Art Gallery
Tate Britain
Tate Modern*
Victoria & Albert Museum*
Victoria & Albert Museum of Childhood
Whitechapel Gallery
Wallace Collection

*Reviewed in *Clued In London*

Other [Free] Sights found in our pages:

Harrods
Trafalgar Square
Shoreditch neighborhood
Borough Market
Piccadilly Circus
Jermyn Street
Big Ben "The Elizabeth Tower"
Chinatown

Official "Bank" Holidays in Great Britain:

New Year's Day
Good Friday
Easter Sunday
Easter Monday
Mayday Monday
End of May Monday
End of August Monday
Christmas Day (Dec. 25)
Boxing Day (Dec. 26)

Major Festivals and Special Events

New Year's Day Parade
This huge parade has marched through the
streets of the Westminster neighborhood since 1987.
Held annually on January 1st

The Boat Race
This historic tradition pits England's best
rowers against each other on the River Thames.
Scheduled during the last week of March/first week of April

London Marathon
Runners traverse London from three different starting
points in this world famous long distance competition.
Usually held on the last Sunday in April

Changing of the Guard - Buckingham Palace
This colorful ceremony lasts about 45 minutes,
in front of the palace gates.
*Usually everyday at 11:30am but double-check online.
It is held when weather permits.*

Chelsea Flower Show
This famous flower show attracts
visitors from all over the world.
Held annually in May

Wimbledon
Strawberry desserts and strict player dress-codes
define the world's oldest tennis competition.
Held annually in late June & early July

The Proms
Since 1895, this respected cultural event at the
Royal Albert Hall attracts world class conductors and
orchestras. The grand finale, *Last Night of the Proms*,
is the most coveted performance.
Held for eight weeks in late summer

London Film Festival
View the most current films in London's
Southbank neighborhood.
Held annually in mid October

Lord Mayor's Show
Since the 1500's, this has been London's
most elaborate parade procession with fireworks.
This very popular event begins selling tickets in June.
Held annually in late October or early November

Bonfire Night
London's largest fireworks spectacular.
Can be viewed throughout central London.
Held annually on the evening of November 5th

New Year's Eve Celebration
One of London's biggest party nights,
with fireworks along the River Thames
Held annually on December 31st

The LGBTQ Scene

London is a gay-friendly city and so we're including some clubs and bars that you might check out if you're so inclined. But whether you're gay or not, you'll probably have a blast at any of the places on this list. (Gay Pride weekend is traditionally held over the last weekend in June.)

Many bars and pubs close at midnight or before, so call ahead to find out their current seasonal hours of operation. *Calling from within London requires only the main eight digit number. Calling these from the US or Canada will need a (011) before the entire number.*

G-A-Y Bar
Three floors, chic basement area,
Cheap drinks Monday to Thursday
30 Old Compton Street, London
Local mobile calling: 020 7494 2756

The Village Soho
Busy place, Tuesday all night happy hour,
Saturday night go-go boys
81 Wardour Street, London
Local mobile calling: 020 7478 0530

Admiral Duncan
Traditional gay pub,
Most Historic gay venue
Closed Sunday and Monday
54 Old Compton Street, London
Local mobile calling: 020 7437 5300

The Duke of Wellington
Friendly gay pub,
Popular with locals in the neighborhood
77 Wardour Street, London
Local mobile calling: 020 7439 1274

Rupert Street
A crowded and popular bar
Food during the day,
Early evening party crowd
50 Rupert Street, London
Local mobile calling: 020 7494 3059

Circa Soho
Sunday night campiness!
Stylish and chill, great for a pre-club meet up
62 Frith Street, London
Local mobile calling: 020 7734 6826

The Yard
Private courtyard, great for smokers
Entrance across from Rupert Street Bar
Serving food from noon to around 8pm
2 for 1 cocktails on some evenings
57 Rupert Street, London
Local mobile calling: 020 7437 2652

Tipping Clues

London restaurants are fairly straightforward in regard to their guest checks and usually add a gratuity of around 12% to the total. This will be clearly listed, but if it's not then a voluntary tip of 12% to the wait staff is customary if the service was good.   Here are the guidelines for everything else:

Porter: Zero

Doorman: Zero

Taxi driver: Round up, or give £2 - £4 if you have luggage

Tour Guides: £5 to £10 - optional

Hairstylist: 10% if extremely pleased - optional

Theatre Ushers: Zero

Waiters: 12% if it's not already on the guest check

Maitre d's: Zero

Café counters: Zero

Money Clues

- Some banks and credit card companies still appreciate a phone call to let them know you'll be traveling abroad.

- Find out what your daily withdrawal limit is *in British Pounds* so that you don't think your bank card has been rejected at a London ATM when it's actually because you merely tried to take out too much in the same day.

- American debit cards will work fine at Britain's ATM's but be careful about taking out too much cash. London is suddenly a cashless city and you'll find very few places that accept it. Weird, right?

- For the best exchange rate, get your cash out of an ATM that is located at or owned by an actual bank, such as the *Bank of London,* rather than one that is operated by a private money "exchange" company; their ATM machines look just like the bank's in order to deceive you, so go by the name that's advertised on it. Definitely be aware of the ones called "Euronet" because their rates are downright criminal.

- Use up all those British coins by the end of your visit because they are not exchangeable back to dollars no matter how many you have.

- Hotel Tax: In London, hotels may charge a small room per person, per night. This is customarily paid directly to the hotel when you check-out, so be aware.

- Use your bank's debit card for purchases wisely. Since there may be a fee with each use, you might not want to debit that £3 ice cream. The fee will be more than the cone! Try to find a travel-friendly fee-free credit card before your trip.

- You may be eligible for a VAT partial-tax refund on certain purchases. Always take your passport with you when you go to do any major shopping as it will be required during the process. Ask the sales associate to file the digital application (if available) right to your credit or debit card so that your refund is automatic. This way you won't have to do anything at the airport and can proceed right to your departure gate. *Note: You will not receive a VAT refund for any items that you ship home.)*

Telephone Clues

Telephone numbers in London are usually eight digits long, and are written as two sets of four. The country code for the UK is 44, and the area code for London is 20.

Calling London from the US or Canada:
Dial 011- 44, then the area code 20,
plus the eight digit telephone number

Calling London from within London *on a mobile phone:*
Dial 020, and then the eight digit telephone number (eleven digits total)

Calling London from within London *on a landline:*
Dial only the eight digit telephone number

Calling the US from London:
Dial 001 - plus the specific area code,
then the seven digit telephone number

Calling Canada from London:
Dial 001 – plus the city code and then the phone number

Note:

011 is the overseas indication when calling **from** the US or Canada…

001 is the overseas indication when calling **to** the US or Canada

Safety and Common Sense

London is obviously not a crime-free city; it's a real city with eight million residents. But that doesn't mean you'll feel unsafe there. Quite the contrary, especially when referring to central London. Just stay on your guard because a bit of caution and common sense can go a long way. Protect your valuables the same way you would anywhere, by using the electronic safe in your hotel room and by keeping money tucked away out of sight. And never leave your luggage unattended out front of your hotel.

Like any place with lots of visitors there's an increased chance of being pick-pocketed, especially in crowded areas like in the Tube system or at popular sights. Ladies: close and fasten your handbag. Men: keep your wallet anywhere except your back pocket.

Bottles, bottles, everywhere... Should you help out the environment by foregoing the plastic and asking your waiter for tap water instead? Of course you should. London's water tastes great and is completely safe to drink. So unless you want fizzy water, tap is the way to go. And it's free in any café or restaurant.

Bathrooms in London establishments are a privilege, not a right. If you wish to use one, you'll be expected to buy something first. There are many hotels in central London, and the larger ones will almost have a men's and women's loo right in the lobby area. Feel free to duck inside.

If you should find yourself unwell for any reason, visit one of London's many pharmacy drug stores- most are large and open late. Your hotel can call a medical professional for you if required, which is another good reason to stay at a full service hotel rather than in a private apartment.

Emergency? Dial 999

Established in 1936, it's the oldest emergency phone number in the world!

The UK has a different electrical current than the U.S., and to make matters more difficult, the plug style (and shape) that allows you to connect to an electrical outlet is even different between London and Paris. This means you need to be prepared. Take a couple of plug adaptors with you, the more the better. Don't worry, they're cheap and can be ordered on amazon.com which is much easier than running all over town trying to find them. Plan in advance!

We don't recommend taking *electrical converters* with you because we don't trust them. They rarely work on things like blow dryers, even though the companies making them claim that they will convert the electrical current on any appliance. Most decent hotels supply a blow dryer for you because it's cheaper than paying to repair that burned room.

As for your iPhone, laptop, or other high-tech toy…they're already made dual-voltage so the only thing you need to worry about is getting that plug adapter so you can actually plug it in!

Your Embassy

If for any reason you feel you need to reach out to your embassy, (passport problems, safety, legal problems, etc.) here is the necessary information:

American Embassy in London:
Local London mobile call: 020 7499 9000
Intl. calling from the US: (011) 44-20 7499 9000
-Located at 33 Nine Elms Lane, London
SU117US United Kingdom

Canadian Embassy in London:
Local London mobile call: 020 7004 6000
Intl. calling from Canada: (011) 44-20 7004 6000
-Located at Canada House at Trafalgar Square, London
SW1Y5BJ United Kingdom

From the Authors

We've had a great time bringing this book to you and sincerely hope you found it useful. The star rating offered to you at the end is for metadata use only and does not affect our online stars. If you enjoyed *Clued In London*, please take a moment to leave a short customer review on Amazon.com so that your rating will count for us. Even a few sentences would be greatly appreciated.

Our blog is easily accessible and offers additional information to travelers between our annual updates. We also field any and all questions, comments, advice, and suggestions at **cluedintravelbooks@gmail.com.**

If you're looking for experiences that will take your British visit to the next level, check out our super fun *Bored in London*, now in ebook and print at **www.amazon.com/dp/B09MR8X2XV**

Thank you so much for your support. Check out our other cool *Clued In* travel books, all exclusively on Amazon.

Clued In Edinburgh
Clued In Venice
Clued in Rome
Clued In Florence
Clued In Barcelona
Clued in Paris
Clued In Miami
Clued In New York
Clued In San Francisco

For more information on this or other
© Clued In travel books, visit our city-by-city blog at
www.cluedintravelbooks.com

Made in United States
Orlando, FL
18 March 2023

31163829R00109